One person had qu

"He's Huge, my lord
palace!"

As the messenger spoke of the strange creature who had suddenly appeared out of nowhere in the counties north of the palace, the courtiers gathered in the royal chambers of Gepeth shook their heads in shocked astonishment.

"He can crush a house just by stepping on it!" the messenger continued.

The courtiers gasped.

"When his giant arms wave up and down, whole villages are blown over! The next morning, the plum trees are all bare — and the few plums we find on the ground have no skin left on them!"

The courtiers paled. Their eyes widened in fear, and their breathing almost stopped.

But one person in the room had quite a different reaction. *Her* eyes sparkled. *Her* face was flushed with excitement. *She* could hardly remain in her seat. It was the Princess Lenora, and anyone could see that she was delighted by everything she heard.

Travel to new dimensions.
Read

⟨ POINT FANTASY ⟩

Of Two Minds
by Carol Matas and Perry Nodelman

Princess Nevermore
by Dian Curtis Regan

Shadow of the Red Moon
by Walter Dean Myers

The Enchanted Forest Chronicles
Dealing with Dragons
Searching for Dragons
Calling on Dragons
Talking to Dragons
by Patricia C. Wrede

Book of Enchantments
by Patricia C. Wrede

MORE MINDS

+ + + ⟨ POINT FANTASY ⟩ + + +

MORE MINDS

CAROL MATAS

AND

PERRY NODELMAN

SCHOLASTIC INC.
New York Toronto London Auckland Sydney

ISBN 0-590-39469-X

12 11 10 9 8 7 6 5 4 3   8 9/9 0 1 2 3/0

Printed in the U.S.A.   01

First Scholastic printing, June 1998

This book is dedicated to those who visited Gepeth and the lands nearby before we did, and showed us the way—with a special thanks to Frank and Charlie.

MORE MINDS

1

"He's huge, my lord! He's taller than this whole palace!"

As the messenger spoke of the strange creature who had suddenly appeared out of nowhere in the counties north of the palace, the courtiers gathered in the royal chambers of Gepeth shook their heads in shocked astonishment.

"He can crush a house by just stepping on it!" the messenger continued.

The courtiers gasped.

"When his giant arms wave up and down, whole villages are blown over! The next morning, the plum trees are all bare—and the few plums we find on the ground have no skin left on them!"

The courtiers paled. Their eyes widened in fear, and their breathing almost stopped.

But one person in the room had quite a different reaction. *Her* eyes sparkled. *Her* face was flushed with excitement. *She* could hardly remain in her seat. It was the Princess Lenora, and anyone could see that she was delighted by everything she heard.

As the messenger finished his tale, King Rayden nodded sympathetically. "Have you tried imagining him away?" he asked. "That *is* allowed in exceptional circumstances. Am I not right, Agneth?"

He turned to the tall, thin, balding man who stood near him.

"As Keeper of the Balance, my lord," said the tall man in a dry, serious voice as he rose to his feet, "I would of course prefer that I be consulted first. But in exceptional circumstances . . ."

"Well, these certainly sound like exceptional circumstances to me," the king interrupted. "And it is the way we usually deal with these sorts of problems, isn't it?" The king made a little sideways glance at Lenora, who was usually the one who *caused* the problems—and frowned as he noticed her happy grin.

"Oh, yes, of course, my lord," the messenger said. "We tried that—" he turned to Agneth and made a slight bow— "begging your pardon, sir keeper. I know we should have consulted you first, but our local subkeeper, Indrang, thought it wise to act at once." Agneth gave the messenger an imperious and unhappy stare. The messenger turned back to the king.

"We did our best, my lord," he continued. "The leaders of all three northern counties gathered, and they put their minds together and imagined that the giant wasn't there—that he simply didn't exist at all anymore. But it didn't work. The giant was munching on a snack at that moment—one of our rare Kitznoldian pear trees it was, and very valuable—and he was completely untroubled by our efforts. Just kept right on munching. When we finally looked up, it was the pear tree that had disappeared—down his gullet, curse him!"

Lenora could stand it no longer. "Father," she rushed over and knelt down before the king, "I can do it! I know I can! Let *me* go after him!"

King Rayden glared at his daughter, trying to keep his temper, while Queen Savet looked at her in worried dismay. Agneth, the keeper, stared at the ceiling and shook his head sadly. But the biggest reaction came from Lenora's fiancé,

Prince Coren. He rose to his feet, his pale cheeks flushing to match the red freckles that covered them.

"No, Lenora," he insisted. "No! Not again." Had she already forgotten the horrible mess she'd ending up making the last time she used her imagination to solve a problem? That business with Hevak, in the land of Grag—why, she'd nearly done in Coren himself for good. Not to mention the entire known universe. Surely she had learned her lesson?

Well, obviously she hadn't. The look she gave him was so cold he actually found himself shivering.

"Anyway," he added lamely, shrinking under her glare, "we have a holiday planned, don't we?"

"Really, Coren," Lenora said, her voice as icy as her look, "how can you think of holidays when a horrible giant is terrorizing our land?"

Our land? Well, Coren thought, as he sank back into his chair, it clearly wasn't the time to correct her, but it was *her* land, not *his*. Not yet, anyway, not until he and Lenora were actually married. Why, if that giant had shown up back home in Andilla, no one would even have known it was there. The Andillans were all too busy living in their imaginations, constantly communicating with one another mentally, constantly thinking up new realities inside their heads and acting as if they were real. They were all so busy mentally making mush taste like dragon flambé and mentally transforming lumpy mattresses into feather duvets filled with floating angel wings that they wouldn't even have noticed something as unexciting as a giant.

Which was why Coren preferred Lenora's country. Here in Gepeth everything was what it appeared to be, solid, reliable. Real.

Oh, the inhabitants could change that, of course. They all had that accursed ability of Lenora's to change their reality to anything they imagined, whenever and however they felt like imagining it. It was a much scarier ability than that of his own people, whose fantasy ideas became real only in their own minds. But most of the time, thank goodness, the Gepethians simply chose not to use their powers. They had made Gepeth just the way they wanted it—and now that it was perfect, they just kept it that way forever. The Balance, they called it and they had that bossy councillor, Agneth the keeper, and a whole bunch of other subkeepers specially assigned to make sure people kept it properly. Coren felt it was all very sensible.

But Lenora, as usual, wanted things to be different. Why couldn't she be as wise as the rest of the Gepethians? As he glanced at her flushed cheeks, his heart sank.

Lenora had been very good since their return from that other world, Grag, where she'd nearly disappeared him and everybody else out of existence. In the weeks since then she hadn't created anything.

Well, not much of anything—only harmless things, really, like the small private waterfall and pond she conjured up for them to swim in. Oh, and there *was* the arbor she'd produced at the back of the palace grounds where they could sit for hours and talk and no one could find them. And sometimes there were little treats to eat. A special chocolate pie or a perfect nectarine would appear by his bedside, a tasty snack just before he went to sleep. There was nothing wrong with *that*, surely?

This, however, was quite a different matter. Rushing off toward a dangerous giant. Any sensible person would be heading off in the other direction, *away* from the giant.

And now Lenora was frowning, and flaring her nostrils. A bad sign, a very bad sign.

"I forbid it, Lenora," King Rayden was saying, "I absolutely

4 ◆

forbid it. The very idea of rushing off after a monster is ridiculous, when all we have to do is imagine it out of existence. And we can do that from here, of course, in the comfort of our own palace. All we have to do is find enough strong-minded people who have been to the north counties so that they have a clear picture of it in their head. I've been there myself, once or twice. We'll gather together here and think of the north counties *without* the giant, and we'll quickly disappear this big thing—assuming Agneth approves? Keeper?"

"I do, my lord," the keeper said. "Giants are forbidden. He has to go. We must do what we must do—even use our powers. Gather your group, my lord. I, meanwhile, will be in the chapel addressing the Pillars, begging forgiveness, doing what I can to keep the Balance intact."

The king nodded, then continued speaking to Lenora. "And *you*, my dear child, will stay out of it. You have other things to worry about right now." He turned toward Coren and winked slyly at him.

"A wise decision indeed, my lord," Agneth announced. Lenora glared at the keeper, daggers in her eyes.

"I wonder where it came from," Queen Savet mused as she looked up from her embroidery. "How could something we didn't create appear, just like that, in *our* country? Unless—" She paused and turned toward Lenora, a questioning look on her face. At the same moment, the king and Agneth turned toward Lenora, too.

Yes, Lenora thought, not noticing their stares. That was exactly why she had wanted to go and see this giant thing so badly. How *could* it manage to exist at all, in a country where a boring fool like Agneth was in charge, where everything was so controlled, where every single person had just totally forgotten about the ability to create whatever wonderful world they wanted, where every single person just agreed to the one, same, boring, horrible, endless reality all the time, so that everything was always the same and nothing ever happened and no one was ever allowed to have any fun!

At least *she* never was. Why, the biggest dose of excitement she'd had in the last few weeks was deciding whether to create a chocolate pie or a strawberry sundae for Coren as a secret bedtime snack—and she wouldn't even have had the fun of doing that if bedtime snacks weren't collectively frowned upon in Gepeth because of some dumb theory about them giving you nightmares.

The snacks *had* given both her and Coren nightmares. So what? What was wrong with nightmares anyway? At least they were interesting.

And Coren *had* eaten the forbidden pie. So now he'd *have* to agree to this, too.

Lenora turned to look at him. His red hair and freckles, his high cheekbones and full mouth could make him look terribly handsome at some times and like some silly clown at others. Right now, with his mouth turned down and his face so pale, he looked more like the latter.

"Oh, Coren, stop it," she whispered, as she plunked herself back down in the chair beside him. "I won't make you come with me if you don't want to."

"I *don't* want to!" Coren whispered back. "I've had enough adventures for a lifetime, believe me. And I don't want you to go either, Lenora. It's dangerous. And what about our trip to the Islands, to see if they'd be a suitable place to live after we're married?"

"Honestly, Coren," Lenora declared, loud enough to attract

the stares of some of the courtiers seated nearby. They were trying to follow the king's conversation with Agneth about how exactly to deal with the giant, and they glared at her angrily.

Impatiently, she shook her head, then leaned toward Coren and whispered in his ear. "There may be no Islands left for us to go to," she said, "if someone doesn't do something about this giant creature. And you know as well as I that I'm probably the most powerful mind here. They need *me*, even if they won't admit it."

"They won't admit it," Coren whispered back, "because they love you and don't want you to get hurt! And neither do I. Why can't you leave it at that?"

She glared at him then, and her green eyes sparkled. She pushed her long blond hair out of her eyes and he had to allow that excitement agreed with her. She looked better than she had in weeks.

"I *can* help and I'm *going* to help," she hissed, "whether they like it or not! Whether *you* like it or not."

Coren's heart sank. Once Lenora made up her mind to do something, that was that.

"They'll never let you go," he warned her. "This time they'll set guards to watch you. You know they don't approve of traveling—your mother isn't even all that happy about this little trip to the Islands. And they certainly don't approve of going on adventures! And you can bet they haven't forgotten what happened in Grag."

Lenora, who had just stood up, sank back into her chair. Coren was right. After that interesting visit she'd made to Hevak's country they knew what she was capable of, and they obviously didn't trust her. This time, they would take no chances. If her father and that meddling fool Agneth decided they didn't want her to go on this expedition, they would make sure she didn't go. She folded her arms and suddenly grew very quiet.

King Rayden, who had been watching her and Coren out of the corner of his eye, nodded. Hopefully Lenora had realized how reckless her scheme was. That boy was a good, stable influence on her, no doubt about it. The sooner they were married the better for everybody.

But Coren himself looked at Lenora's calm expression and became even more alarmed. He knew she was plotting something. In fact, he now realized in surprise, he could overhear her thinking about it.

"They *can't* stop me," she fumed. "There must be a way . . ."

Coren had promised Lenora that he'd stay out of her head—it made her furious, absolutely furious, when he used the powers of his people and read her thoughts. As well it should, Coren thought. He'd always hated it when people back home in Andilla did it to him, and he'd made a resolution to himself never to use his powers if he could possibly help it.

But sometimes he couldn't help it. He found himself hearing Lenora's thoughts despite himself, because her mind was so strong, so intense. He closed his eyes and made a determined effort to block out her thoughts. An image of a huge chocolate pie filled his head.

By the time he erased the pie and opened his eyes again, Lenora was smiling sweetly at her father. "Coren's right," she said aloud into a lull in the official conversation. "We really can't delay our trip to the Islands, can we? And that's an adventure all in itself! I mean, a real trip, to a different place! I suppose you'll have to do it without me."

What? Coren was almost sorry he'd blotted her scheming

out of his mind. "Lenora," he whispered, "what are you up to?"

"Nothing," she said through her teeth, not even looking at him as she smiled at her father. "Nothing at all." Then, her voice suddenly very sweet and very gentle, she said, "All this talk of giants has made me feel queasy, Father. Would you mind if I went to my room?"

King Rayden was so preoccupied with making plans to get rid of the giant that he just waved her away, forgetting that Lenora *never* got queasy—and never asked his permission for anything.

Lenora rose, smiled yet again, and smoothly swept out of the ballroom.

2

Once in the corridor, Lenora's smile immediately turned into an angry frown. "Blast," she exclaimed. Then she stalked back toward her room, barely noting the servants scrambling to get out of her way or Coren calling after her as he desperately tried to catch up.

"Honestly," she muttered to herself as she walked. "This place is impossible! A monster to be seen, an adventure just waiting to happen—and everyone just stays here and—and thinks! They're all stuck here, like . . . like . . . like carrots rooted in the ground!"

"Lenora, wait!"

She turned on Coren roundly. "You—you carrot!"

"Carrot?" Coren pulled up beside her, panting a little.

"Yes, carrot! Stuck here forever, just like all the other carrots. You'd rather be planted here vegetating than off seeing the world. Why don't you admit it and let me go have my adventures?"

"I *do* admit it," he said. "Why wouldn't I? I'm not ashamed of it, and I don't see why I should be. What's wrong with vegetating, as you call it? There's no place like home, Lenora. And once we're married, well, if I want to stay home and see to the meals and the linen and you want to head the hunting parties or travel about on the circuit court settling disputes, we can do it. They can't stop us, once we're married. That's what I've been trying to tell you for weeks now."

"I know," she sighed, and she permitted him to walk beside her as she continued on to her rooms. He wasn't brave but he could be quite lovable. It was hard to be angry with him for very long.

"And," she added, "that's the *only* reason I agreed to this marriage."

"The only one?" Coren said, his eyes downcast.

At that she stopped in her tracks, turned, pulled him to her, and kissed him fiercely.

"Not the *only* one," she grinned, as they came up for air. Then she let go of him and, having reached her rooms, entered and promptly slammed the door in his face.

"Now go away," she shouted through the door. "I have to think. And," she added, "don't you dare try to read my mind, either. I can feel it when you do!"

It was a tickling sensation inside her head. *Very* annoying.

She looked around the room, suddenly dissatisfied with everything. It was so *blue*. A large blue canopy bed, a plush blue chair by the fireplace, a solid wood wardrobe painted royal blue, pale blue walls. She was so tired of boring old blue. How could she ever have chosen blue as her favorite color? It had to go.

In a flash, she was standing in a forest of rich oranges and reds. The bed was gone, and the floor was covered in a thick carpet of zinnias and marigolds. Actual flowers, not just images of them—why not? She lay down in the flowers and gazed at the ceiling, which gave the appearance of fluffy orange clouds in a rich crimson sky.

"Now *this* is interesting," she sighed. "Why can't things be like this all the time?"

As she absently observed one of the clouds that was drifting across the bright red sky, she began to play one of her old childhood games—imagining what sort of thing the cloud looked like and then making it really be that thing.

"Rabbit," she said aloud, "fuzzy green rabbit." A green creature with large floppy ears hopped down from the sky and hid among the orange trees.

Then, "Little girl, happy little girl running wherever she wants." As Lenora watched, the little girl skipped from orange cloud to orange cloud, singing a jolly song about the sunshine. She looked just like Lenora—but much younger, and much, much happier.

I should pluck her down, Lenora thought idly, and let her live here with all these dreary carrot people. Then she'd stop being so ridiculously happy. As Lenora thought this, the little girl changed, grew older and more serious. Now she looked just like Lenora herself. She sat on the edge of a cloud, her feet dangling, staring morosely down at her double on the floor below.

Suddenly Lenora sat bolt upright. Her room, without her imagining it differently, returned to normal, and both the girl and the cloud she was sitting on blinked out of sight. Lenora herself was now sitting on the cold hardwood floor, but she didn't feel it.

Why not? she thought. Why can't I just create *another* me? Another Lenora! I'll make her exactly like me in every way. Same face, same hair, same body, same memories—no one will ever realize she *isn't* me. And she can take my place while I do what I want! Oh, it's so obvious! Why didn't I ever think of this before? I'll be off having fun giant hunting, and she'll be the one who's sitting around here being bored or going to the stupid Islands with Coren and counting the stupid towels there.

At this thought, Lenora's brow wrinkled a little. Someone else on the island with Coren. Someone else holding his hand and sharing his secrets and—

But it was ridiculous to worry about it. It'd be herself, after all, more or less. She could hardly be jealous of herself.

And it was such a good idea—too good not to try. Not only would she have the adventure of meeting the giant, but she'd finally actually get to see Gepeth.

But I must do it now, she told herself. If I don't leave right away, Father will gather his stupid thinking party together and get rid of the giant and spoil all the fun.

"I'll do it," she declared.

Lenora gazed at herself in the mirror. She fixed her own image in her mind, both physically and mentally, then closed her eyes and gave a push of energy. When she opened her eyes, there were two people staring at the mirror, instead of one.

It was herself. There were two of her now.

As Lenora turned to look at the new her standing beside her, the new Lenora did the exact same thing. "This is odd, isn't it?" they both said at the same time. At exactly the same time—which was when Lenora realized that the other Lenora was indeed exactly like her.

It was creepy. Very creepy.

And it meant that the other Lenora must have all her powers. Another mind, just like hers. What if the new Lenora tried to get rid of the *original* Lenora?

Oh, this hadn't been such a good idea after all!

"I'm afraid you'll have to go," Lenora said. And she heard the words echo as she spoke them.

Terrified, she immediately thought her other self away—and for one horrible second, she felt *herself* actually flickering, on the verge of winking out of existence all together.

Then the moment passed, and her power surged through her, and she was alone again. She looked up to see just one Lenora looking back at her from the mirror.

As she stood there shaking with relief, she realized what a terrible mistake she'd almost made. What if her wish—*their* wish—had worked, and both of them had actually managed to disappear each other? She'd be gone for good.

It had been a close call, all right. This was going to take some careful thinking. She had to create a Lenora who looked like her, talked like her, but didn't *think* like her.

How could a person *talk* like you, if they didn't *think* like you?

And then there was Coren. He could read minds, after all. If the new Lenora didn't think like the original one, then Coren would know it wasn't her right away, even if nobody else suspected.

Well, maybe not *right* away. She had him pretty well trained, and he did at least try to stay out of her head. If she was lucky he wouldn't suspect anything until after she'd replaced herself with the substitute and left. And even when he did realize she was thinking differently—why would he jump to the conclusion it wasn't really her? After all, as he was always informing her in no uncertain terms, he already thought she was kind of wacky and inconsistent and hard to understand. To him, nothing about her would be any different.

So, how could she make a Lenora that was her—and wasn't her?

Well, first of all, she told herself, remembering how strange it had felt as she looked into her own eyes, the new Lenora can't know about me. And if what just happened means anything, I'll have to try to keep away from her myself. So I'll have to imagine her into existence somewhere else—not here with me.

And somewhere where the new Lenora will be happy—too happy to do any thinking about how she got there and start asking embarrassing questions.

Happy! That's it, Lenora told herself. I'll make her happy! She'll be happy with all the things that bore me! I'll fill her head with china patterns and kitchen equipment and towels!

Lenora smiled, imagining the look on the face of Fullbright, the old retainer Queen Savet had put in charge of the wedding, when he saw that Lenora was, for the first time, actually paying attention to all his talk about organdy versus taffeta, and seriously considering the virtues of pale green over medium green ribbons. Fullbright *loved* all that nonsense, and Lenora had done nothing to hide her boredom from him.

Oh, yes, Lenora told herself, Fullbright will be just mad about the new me—so much so he won't even realize I'm not behaving like the old me.

In fact, why not make the new Lenora into what *everybody* had always wanted her to be? Everybody's dream Lenora— calm, placid, obedient. They'd be so busy being delighted by how agreeable and how wonderful she suddenly was, they wouldn't even stop to think about why it happened or what it meant! Even that annoying fool, Agneth, wouldn't be able to find fault with her.

And so, slowly, carefully, Lenora imagined a Lenora who looked just like her but who had thoughts like those of a compliant child—a Lenora with a different mind. She closed her eyes. She concentrated. And then she made what she saw real.

Or so she hoped. She couldn't exactly go check and see if the other Lenora was now in a meeting with Fullbright, as

Lenora had imagined. But she didn't see why she wouldn't be. Lenora was a master of creating what she imagined. She clapped her hands in glee and did a little dance.

Realizing that she didn't have long before people began to notice she was in two places at once, she cut short her little celebration and readied herself to leave.

It was an easy thing to do. She didn't need to pack, because now that nobody would be around to watch her, she could create anything she needed as she traveled. And the same principle applied to food.

She dressed in a loose shift and a comfortable pair of sandals as if she were just going for a walk in the woods. Then she caught her hair up in a twist and fixed it with a brown leather clasp. And that was it. She was ready.

She opened the door to find Coren standing just outside.

"How long have you been here?" she demanded.

"Too long," he grumbled. He paused. "I don't trust you, Lenora. You're up to something."

"Have you been in my mind?" she accused, genuinely worried. If he had been, her clever plan was doomed.

"No! No! I haven't," he assured her. "I wouldn't! I just didn't like the look on your face before."

"Well, you're right," Lenora smiled, heaving a sigh of relief inside. "I *was* mad. I still am, I guess. But I don't know how to convince them to let me go, so I suppose I'll have to leave it for now."

That sounds pretty convincing, she thought, but I'd better add something to it. He'll never believe I could give up so easily.

"Actually, to tell the truth, well—" she produced a nervous little laugh, and hoped she sounded embarrassed—"I just need more time to figure out how to change Father's mind. I think

I'll take a walk—alone, Coren—and mull it over. Tell you what. I'll meet you at Fullbright's office in half an hour. Remember we were supposed to go over those stupid invitations with him?"

Coren looked *very* relieved.

"Are you sure?" he said.

"Yes, positive. Just give me a while to think things over."

Coren looked at her. She *seemed* sincere. Still, there was something tugging at him. . . . She'd given in too easily. It wasn't like her, not at all.

Unless—unless she was actually beginning to *change*! Maybe that was it. Maybe she was losing her need for constant adventure. Maybe she was finally getting ready to settle down.

If only. Coren doubted it, somehow.

He accepted the peck on the cheek Lenora gave him and watched her run off down the hall. Well, he'd give her the benefit of the doubt. Why shouldn't he? After all, it was only a few minutes. And if they were to be married their union would have to be based on trust. Might as well start now.

And he was proud of himself for *not* listening in on her thoughts. Very proud.

There was still half an hour to kill before the meeting with Fullbright. Coren decided to go back to the conference in the banquet hall and see how the plans to deal with the giant were progressing.

He arrived just as the council was breaking up.

"So it's agreed," the king was saying. "As soon as the twenty people we've chosen are prepared, we'll gather right here in the royal chambers and put our minds together. With all that power unleashed at once, we'll disappear this big lug in no time at all."

As the councillors left the room, murmuring and nodding to

one another, the king caught sight of Coren. "Ah, Prince Coren," he said, "you've come back. Has Lenora calmed down?"

"Yes, sir," Coren said. Well, it was true—and no point getting Rayden all worried about his vague suspicions, which was really all they were.

"Good, good," the king said, giving him a hearty clap on the back. But he must have noticed the concern on Coren's face. "Now don't you worry, my lad," he added. "This isn't your problem. You just concentrate on your wedding plans. Take Lenora on that little trip to the Islands—I'll talk Savet into it, just you wait and see. Yes, indeed, it'd be the best thing for all of us."

Coren was relieved. There was nothing to worry about. He'd get Lenora out of harm's way, and King Rayden and his team of powerful minds would take care of everything else.

But, Coren had to admit to himself, he was a little surprised that Rayden hadn't remembered his ability to read thoughts. Surely the king wanted to know where the monster came from and how it got there? And if he had asked Coren to read its mind . . .

But what did it matter where it came from if they could so easily just get rid of it? Rayden didn't need Coren. There was obviously no point in even bringing up the idea.

So Coren merely thanked King Rayden for the information and headed for Fullbright's office to await Lenora there.

4

To Coren's surprise, Lenora was already there when he arrived. She was sitting demurely to the left of Fullbright on a small settee, nodding and smiling as he turned the pages of an album of wedding invitations and spoke of their relative merits.

In the few moments since he'd last seen her, Coren noticed that Lenora had managed to change both her clothes *and* her hair. She was wearing a gown he'd never seen before—a long, full-skirted one in deep mauve, covered with pink ribbons and lace. And her hair was hanging loose, but somehow it seemed to have developed waves and curls. In fact, she looked absolutely stunning.

"Hello," Coren said, uncertainly.

Lenora looked up at the sound of his voice. As she caught sight of him, her eyes began to sparkle, and her mouth widened into a huge smile.

"Oh, Coren, darling!" she exclaimed. She leaped up from her seat and threw her arms around him. "My dear, darling husband to be! I've missed you, sweetums!"

Sweetums?

"Come, dear, sit down." She took his hand and guided

him across the room and sat him directly across from her. "You must see all these wonderful invitations. Look at this one, with the raised silver bells and the italic lettering—isn't it just divine!"

Divine?

"And, oh, Coren, Fullbright has been giving me the most wonderful ideas for the wedding! I don't know why I couldn't see it before. I was simply being too stubborn for words! Why, if I'd just taken two seconds to *listen*, we wouldn't have had to waste so much time. Never mind, though, I see the light now! This is going to be the most glamorous, glittering wedding *ever* given. We'll be the envy of every royal house from here to Benering! I'm leaning toward mauve and pink for the pew ribbons—what do you think, sweetums?"

Pew ribbons? Lenora wanted pink pew ribbons? Now Coren *knew* something was wrong.

"All right, Lenora," he said, "that's enough. Just because I didn't agree with every single one of your crazy ideas doesn't mean you have to be so sarcastic!"

"Why, Coren," Lenora chided, giving him a wide-eyed look of innocence that was almost totally convincing. "How can you accuse me of that? I'm not being the least *bit* sarcastic. I mean it. I think Fullbright is a genius!"

Fullbright, who was round, bald, and pink cheeked, beamed.

"I knew you'd see it my way eventually, Princess," he glowed. "We *will* be the envy of them all!" He sighed happily.

Coren had had enough. Lenora was sitting there smiling at him in a self-satisfied way like a cat over cream, almost as if she were defying him not to believe her silly performance. And pretending to actually notice differences between all those invitations. She probably didn't know an italic letter from a soup tureen.

Well, he'd promised not to enter her head, but if she was going to treat him with such contempt, then he had a right, no, a duty to himself not to be taken advantage of in this way.

He sent his mind out to hers, entered it—and found her considering the advantages of carnations over sprigs of lily of the valley as a wedding bouquet.

No secret plot to humiliate him. No anger. No resentment at her father. Nothing. Not even anything about the giant. Nothing but flowers. Nothing but marriage plans.

And what was even stranger, she didn't seem to notice that he was there. Lately, she'd gotten very sensitive to him, and the few times he *had* entered her mind, she'd caught him. Not right away, but within a minute or so. Now she seemed completely oblivious to his presence.

Embarrassed, he withdrew. This was amazing. Lenora was making wedding plans. Lenora was happy.

He was happy, too. He decided to tell her how pleased he was. "Lenora," he began. "I—"

"Call me Leni," she interrupted. "Lenora is so formal, don't you think? We really *should* have nicknames for each other—it's so cute, don't you think? You call me Leni. And I'll call you Cori!" Then she actually giggled. Giggled. He'd *never* heard her giggle before. Laugh, yes. Snicker, often. Guffaw even. But giggle? Not likely!

"Ooh, Cori," she squealed, "you look so cute when you wrinkle your nose like that. Now don't worry, you'll get used to it soon. What were you going to say?"

Coren looked at her, bewildered. "I forget," he answered.

"Never mind, Cori sweetums," she said, "just listen to what Fullbright has to say about these invitations. I *do* like the italics."

* * *

Fooled *all* of them, Lenora thought with some satisfaction, smiling to herself.

She had walked casually out of the palace, down through the village, and out onto the road to the north counties where the giant was terrorizing everyone. And nobody had even bothered to notice her.

She did have a small twinge about tricking Coren that way. After all, they *were* supposed to trust each other and all that stuff.

Well, then, she thought defiantly, he should have backed me up! Then I *could* have taken him into my confidence. It's his own fault, that's all. His own fault.

And she resolved not to think about him again. There were roads to travel, giants to conquer. She had work to do!

5

As she marched down the gravel road that led away from her home, Lenora began to feel a little bit nervous. She realized she had never before explored any of Gepeth on her own. Come to think of it, she'd hardly been out of the castle or the village in her entire life, except in her imagination. Travel was frowned upon in Gepeth, and most people just stayed home—rooted, they were, exactly like carrots. Except for people traveling on official royal business, strangers hardly ever came to the castle, and the people who lived there hardly ever left it—that's why Queen Savet was so upset by the idea of Coren and Lenora going off to the Islands.

Not that Lenora had ever minded. She was perfectly happy making up different worlds and living in those for her adventures, and it had never occurred to her that there might be anything in the boring, familiar world of Gepeth to investigate. Not with that stupid Balance controlling everything.

But now she was hiking down a road she'd never been on, in her own country, in the world she shared with everybody else—and for some reason it made her nervous. Why?

Finally, the reason came to her. In *her* worlds, the ones she created, she was in control of everything. In this one, she wasn't. The laws and the nature of Gepeth had long been agreed to, and she couldn't just go traipsing through the country changing things at will.

For one thing, if she did, the people would immediately know who she was—because there was no question about it, she had a reputation for that sort of thing. The ordinary Gepethians who came to the court for legal matters or banquets were always asking one of the courtiers to point out the princess with the crazy imagination who kept on trying to spoil their perfect little world. Lenora had often noticed some wide-eyed stranger or other whispering with the courtiers, staring at her with a mixture of awe and fear. One time, she got so fed up with it that she crossed the eyes of one of the strangers. It served him right, too—even if King Rayden made her put them straight again as soon as he found out. No crossed eyes were allowed in his perfect little kingdom, and that was that.

Still, she hadn't felt nervous in a long time. She always knew she could handle everything, but now . . .

Maybe, she thought, I should forget this silly traveling and just imagine myself where that giant is right now. She tried to get an image of the north counties in her head. She knew from experience that you couldn't throw yourself into a place unless you could picture it very clearly in your mind first. That was why the group Rayden planned to gather had to include people who'd been to the North.

But when she thought of the North herself, all Lenora's mind could come up with was some rather wispy mountains with sheep all over them, labeled with words identifying their breed. It was an image from the geography book she'd been forced to read as a child—and a very vague image at that.

Apparently, she hadn't paid nearly enough attention to her geography lessons back then. The image certainly wasn't clear enough to take a gamble on jumping into.

Of course, she thought, I could just imagine the giant away right now, from here, all by myself. I bet my mind is at least as strong as those wimpy councillors of Father's all put together. I'll just tell myself he doesn't exist—and he won't.

But what would be the fun of that?

No, she'd better walk to the north counties after all. Anyway, why not? In fact, she rather liked the feelings she was having. A little fear. A lot of excitement. *This* was living.

She laughed when she thought of the other Lenora happily making wedding plans. They'd all be so pleased with one another, she and Coren and Queen Savet and that silly old Fullbright. They'd be wrangling over ribbons for hours on end. They might even get around to discussing italics, a subject Fullbright kept trying to bring up and Lenora kept avoiding. She had no idea what italics even were, and hoped never to learn. No question about it, she had really put one over on them this time!

As Lenora passed by the carefully cultivated and tended fields, she noticed lots of activity going on—crews of people weeding and hoeing and mowing together as they sang the jolly Gepethian folk songs Lenora had been hearing in the village near her home all her life. And she passed farmers on the road who were driving wagons of hay and other crops and also humming or singing. Sometimes, in between verses, they called out jokes to one another.

Everyone seemed so perfectly happy. It was ridiculous of them to be so happy when everything around them was so boringly normal. For a brief moment, Lenora considered making the crops sing along with everybody else—or maybe creating her own version of the huge giant she was heading for. Anything to shake people up a little.

A lot of the people she passed looked at her curiously for a moment but left her completely alone. They all seemed so determined to go about their daily business without ever doing or saying anything different from what they usually said or did. Even when she called out to say hello to them, they just sort of nodded at her nervously and went back to their work and their singing. Tra la la, tra la lee, on and on.

Finally, Lenora couldn't stand it anymore. She wanted somebody to *notice* her. She stomped over and placed herself in front of a man seated on a horse who was coming toward her from the other direction.

"Excuse me, sir," she said. "I—I seem to be lost."

The man, startled, managed to stop his horse just in front of her, then stared down at her in confusion.

"Lost?" he said. "You can't be lost. This is Gepeth. Everyone always knows exactly where they are and exactly what they are doing. It's the way things are, isn't it? Of course it is. It always has been and always will be, forever and ever and ever. Not that I'm complaining, of course. Praise the Balance. Now stop playing silly schoolgirl games and get out of my way, dear. I have a crop rotation meeting to attend, and everyone else will be on time and will be very upset if you make me late. Nobody in Gepeth is ever late."

The man smiled at her, just as all the rest had—but Lenora was almost positive that she'd detected a hint of bitterness in what he was saying. Surely he couldn't be discontented with perfect life in perfect old Gepeth, where everyone was perfectly happy?

No, of course not, she was imagining things. He was probably irritated at being stopped like that and having his little routine interrupted. She should have known that nobody would believe her if she said she was lost. How could you get lost in a perfect world? Lenora sighed and stepped out of the horse's path, and the man nodded impatiently at her and hurried on his way.

For a while Lenora walked on, listening to the happy singing all around her with an ever-growing annoyance. It was like being held captive by a particularly cheerful opera company.

After a while, her annoyance seemed to spread into the singing itself. It began to sound less happy, somehow—and a little, well, hysterical, as if everyone were merely pretending to be happy and doing their best to hide their real feelings, which were anything but happy.

Could it really be? She listened more carefully and began to pay more careful attention to the people working in the fields near the road. Well, there was no question about it—they were all smiling. Smiling and singing and being jolly enough to make your teeth hurt.

But then she happened to glance at a woman who was carrying a load of weeds she'd just pulled toward a wheelbarrow parked by the side of the road. As Lenora's eyes passed over her, she saw the woman suddenly reach out her foot and give a swift kick to another woman, who was still bent over toward the ground, weeding. A very swift kick—it happened so fast that Lenora wasn't quite sure she'd actually seen it—and both women kept singing and smiling the whole time.

Strange. How could they sound so happy and do something like that? After that, Lenora watched more closely—and noticed a number of other kicks and jabs and quick, angry looks and gestures passing between the workers in the field she passed.

And meanwhile, of course, the happy songs continued.

By now, Lenora was beginning to suspect that nobody at all was as happy as they seemed to be. And yet they were all trying so desperately hard to pretend to be happy—as happy as her father and mother and old Agneth and even her good friend the wise woman, Lufa, had always said everybody in Gepeth was. What was going on here?

Maybe it was the giant they were worried about. Maybe it had put them on edge to have their happy little routines upset by something unusual. That might be it.

She had to find out. At the very next field, she walked up to the first person she came to, a man who was standing beside the heavy plough he'd been pushing. He was panting heavily.

"Bad news about this giant, isn't it?" she said.

"Giant?" the man got out between gasps. "What are you talking about?"

"The giant who's appeared in the north counties."

The man gave her a perplexed look. "Never heard of any giant, miss," he said. "And, anyway, giants don't exist. Not here in good old Gepeth, where everything is always the same and nothing unexpected ever happens. Thank goodness, because I'm certainly not complaining, how could anyone ever want to complain?"

For a moment he stood there, looking at Lenora in obvious bewilderment. Then he shook his head and began to push his plough off into the field.

Lenora stared at his back as he moved away from her, deep in thought. He didn't know about the giant. So this was normal, then. This was just the way things always were in Gepeth.

Things were always the same—and these people, these ordinary Gepethian citizens, they seemed as bored and upset about it as she was herself. Only they were much less willing to admit it. In fact, it seemed to scare them even to realize they were thinking it.

It was nothing like what she'd expected. Nothing like what she'd been told back home in the castle. What could it possibly mean?

6

Well, thinking about it wasn't helping her to find that giant. First things first. Lenora shrugged and continued on down the road.

It had been midday when she started out, and she was beginning to feel more than a little bit hot and tired. She put her hand on the top of her head. Her hair was hot to the touch.

She imagined herself a nice, wide-brimmed straw hat, but quickly realized it was too big and heavy for comfortable walking. Instead, she imagined a soft cotton tam. That was better.

And then some fruit nectar, she thought, *very* cold. A sparkling glass of it appeared in her hand. Perfect. She drank it all, then imagined away the glass.

She walked on for another while, constantly aware of little bursts of anger and discontent that she now felt radiating from the people in the fields. It should have pleased her to know how unhappy some people were, but somehow it didn't. This was Gepeth. Her parents' kingdom—*her* kingdom. It made her feel very uncomfortable. She found herself trying to blot out the discontent in the songs of the people she passed and hear only the happiness.

Finally, Lenora knew she needed a rest. She continued on until she came to a patch of road with no other people in sight—even the constant noise of singing was way off in the distance, so far off it actually did sound cheerful again. And the closest farmhouse was quite far down the road she was traveling.

Good. She could be alone here. Seeing a big old tree by the edge of the road, Lenora plunked herself underneath it. The shade was lovely, and she leaned her head against the rough bark as she ate the dried nectarines that her hunger had caused her to imagine into her hand without even being aware she had done it.

When she got back from defeating the giant, she thought, she'd be able to tell Rayden and Savet how wrong they were about everybody in Gepeth being happy. They trusted their councillors too much—especially that old busybody, Agneth, and his precious Balance. And they'd be so upset to find out what was really happening in the kingdom that they'd be sure to forget to get mad at her for heading off without permission.

And, then, well, they'd have to change things, of course. They'd have to fool around with their precious Balance after all. They'd have to make a world where people could do what they really wanted and everybody *really* would be happy. And she could help! She'd start by making the entire country forget the words of those awful folk songs.

This was turning out to be an even better trip than she'd imagined, she thought, as she dozed off.

When she returned to conciousness, it was probably only minutes later. For some reason she was freezing. Why had it become so cold all of a sudden? And there was something, some kind of powder, on her face. Brushing it off, she opened her eyes and then, shocked at what she saw, jumped to her feet and looked around in total confusion.

Everything had changed. She was standing ankle deep in something white—it was more of the white powder she'd brushed off her face. It was everywhere. White covered the fields, the road, there was white for as far as she could see.

And she was cold, so very cold. The wind, which was the bitterest and fiercest she had ever felt, whipped the white stuff up and blew it across the fields. There were also small particles of it falling from the sky.

She clasped her arms around herself. She was practically frozen. This wouldn't do at all. She'd have to imagine it away.

She did. Nothing happened. The wind kept hurling the painful white particles of cold at her.

Finally, it occurred to her to at least imagine herself into warmer clothing. Thick socks, trousers, leather boots, a wool sweater, and a long, thick wool cape with a hood.

Except, once again, nothing happened. She shivered violently in her thin dress and tried to imagine herself a house, so she could have shelter from the strange storm. But that didn't work, either! She tried again. Still nothing! Her teeth chattered, her body shook.

If I move, that might help keep me warm, she thought. So she began to trudge through the thick white mass, hardly able to comprehend the deep pain of the cold on her bare ankles. The even colder wind howled around her ears. It felt like being stung by a thousand bees all at once. What on earth had happened? Had she been transported to another world?

In the distance she saw a farmhouse and through the white, seething mass of coldness, it looked sort of familiar.

Yes, it was the same one she'd seen earlier, before she fell asleep. So it wasn't another world. She was still in Gepeth. Something was *very* wrong.

She knew she had to get to the farmhouse or she was in terrible danger. Her limbs were beginning to feel numb. Her face was burning. And nothing she thought made things the least bit different. If anything, the wind got stronger and colder.

Why can't I affect this? she thought, in between blasts of wind. I didn't dream it up while I was dozing, I hope.

She didn't think so. How could she imagine something into reality when she'd never seen or even imagined the thing at all? All this cold and wind was certainly not *her* idea. You'd have to be some kind of crackpot to imagine something like this. How could anyone be so foolish as to even imagine living somewhere where *this* happened?

She continued on, slogging through the white stuff, which was getting thicker and thicker. She was able to stay on the road only because it was lined with trees on either side. Without those as markers to tell her which part of the endless sea of white was the road, she knew she could easily end up going around in circles. Her eyes burned and she was starting to feel cold deep, deep inside.

And tired. Almost sleepy. She could see the farmhouse, lights glowing through the swirling mass, getting closer and closer. But it felt like it was taking her forever to get there.

But she kept on slogging, just concentrating on putting one foot in front of the other—and, finally, she could see the house, just to her left in a field of pure, blinding white. She staggered up to the porch, but she couldn't find the steps under the white stuff, and so she just crawled over it, up to the door.

She pounded on the door with all her might and, when it opened, she fell through onto the floor.

"Dear me," she heard a concerned voice say. "Bring her over here by the fire. I'll get her something hot."

And she passed out.

7

Lenora awoke to find herself sitting on a chair beside a blazing fire, wrapped in warm blankets. As she swam into consciousness, she felt a cup being thrust into her hands, but they were too frozen to hold it, and still shaking. Luckily, someone brought the cup to her lips, and she tasted sweet, spiced cider. She sipped it gratefully, feeling it warm her. Eventually she felt warm enough to look around.

Two worried adult faces hovered over her—most likely the farmer and his wife. Four smaller faces of various ages peered at her curiously.

"Look, Mama," one of the children said, pointing to Lenora's hair, which was now dripping. "The white stuff melts in the heat—like butter in a pan."

"So it does," said her mother worriedly. "But it's *not* important. Let's not talk about it." Then she turned to Lenora. "Who are you, my dear?" she asked.

"Le—" She suddenly stopped. She'd almost said her name, and then remembered not to.

"Le?" said one of the children. "That's a funny name." And they all giggled.

"Leteshia," Lenora said. "Leteshia is my name."

It was the name of one of the Pillars of Balance. Lenora had heard Agneth chant the names of the Pillars time and again as he performed his endless weekly ceremonies—so many times that she knew them by heart. "Praise be the Pillars, the stately Socrateen, the magnificent Machiavello, the wise Winichur, the lovely Leteshia." But she'd never really thought much about them. She had no idea who the Pillars actually were, or why their names were said so reverently—only the keeper knew that kind of thing.

As she spoke the name, the children laughed even harder. "That's even funnier!" the same child who had spoken earlier exclaimed. "That's a ceremony name, not a person name!"

"It isn't kind to make fun of someone's name," Lenora reprimanded her. "Just because it's a little different from what you're used to doesn't mean it's silly, you know."

As she said that, the mother looked surprised, then a little shocked. But the child burst into a wide smile. She seemed to be around ten years old. She was thin and wiry, with short brown hair and big brown eyes.

"What's *your* name?" Lenora asked her.

"My name is Sayley," she said. "And I'm sorry I laughed at you, Leteshia. Because you're right. Different *isn't* bad, is it?" She turned and gave her mother a gloating smile—apparently this was a subject they'd discussed before.

The mother glared at the girl and looked even more upset.

"I mean," the child said, her brown eyes sparkling as she turned back toward Lenora, "Sayley is a boring name, half the kids in my school have the same one—the Balance is always making people be Sayley. But Leteshia! Leteshia is— is—delicious!" she finally announced.

"Sayley, that's quite enough," the mother scolded. "You know perfectly well that you love your name just as much as the rest of us do. After all, it was assigned to you by the Balance, wasn't it? Praise the Balance. Sayley is the perfect name for you—as I've told you many, many times before. Now let's not talk about it any more."

"Yes, mother," Sayley said. And then she turned her face toward Lenora so that her mother couldn't see it. "Boring, boring, boring," she whispered to Lenora, and made an ugly grimace.

"And what are you doing here in Bardno County, Leteshia?" the man asked. He looked very suspicious—as if she somehow had something to do with all that white stuff outside.

"I'm traveling to a county in the north," she said.

"Traveling?" His eyes widened. "You mean, going somewhere different? Away from your home county?"

Oh, oh, Lenora thought. For a moment, she'd forgotten how unusual traveling was here in Gepeth.

"I'm on official business from the castle," Lenora explained. "For King Rayden."

"Oh." The man nodded and looked just a little less suspicious.

"But shortly after leaving the castle," Lenora continued, "*that* started outside. What *is* it?"

"We don't know what it is," the woman said. "It's—it's—oh, let's not talk about it."

"We've never seen it before," Sayley chimed in. "Isn't it wonderful?"

"It is, sort of," Lenora said. "Although very cold." She shivered again just thinking about it. "It's different, that's for sure."

"Different!" Sayley exclaimed.

Here was a child with some spunk. Lenora liked her already.

"But what bothers me," Lenora said, "is why it didn't disappear when I tried to imagine it away."

There was a gasp from everybody, then a shocked silence.

"You—you tried to imagine it away?" the man finally asked.

"Yes, of course," Lenora said, "didn't you?" Surely she wasn't the only person in Gepeth who ever tried to use her powers?

But maybe she was. The man paled, then sat down in a chair on the other side of the fire. "I—uh—well, the truth is—" he paused for a long time, apparently summoning up his courage.

"The truth is," he finally mumbled, "yes. I did. I did try to imagine it away."

I thought so, Lenora told herself.

But at his words, the woman gasped again, even louder, and raised her hands to her cheeks. She looked absolutely terrified.

"Yes, Lemilla," he added, turning to look at her, "I *did* try, and you might as well know it."

"Oh, Garfon, Garfon, how could you? Oh. I don't even want to hear about it." She put her hands over her ears.

"I know the castle doesn't like us to," the man went on, leaning toward Lenora with an urgent tone in his voice. "I know that. There's the Balance to think of, isn't there? Praise the blessed Balance forever and ever and ever!"

"Praise the Balance!" his wife murmured, her hands still held firmly over her ears.

"But when something like this happens—" the man paused. "Well," he continued. "It isn't right, is it? And it's our duty as good, upstanding Gepethians to try to restore the Balance—isn't it?" He gazed intently at Lenora, seeking agreement.

"Yes," Lenora nodded, delighted to be able to encourage him. "Of course. You're absolutely and totally right. And I'm sure King Rayden would be happy you feel that way."

The man looked very relieved.

"So," Lenora continued. "Why didn't you do it?"

"I couldn't," he said, looking very confused. "I tried—I did try—and nothing happened." He turned back to Lenora. "I don't seem to have any control over it at all."

"Well, me either," Lenora said. "How peculiar." Then a new thought occurred to her. "Good heavens—does it mean that we've *all* lost our powers?"

"Don't ask me," the woman wailed. "I've never used mine. Never once in my entire life! I swear on the Balance!"

Lenora almost fell off her chair. Being obedient was one thing—but this? "You've *never* used your powers?"

"Of course not," the woman replied. "Why would I? This world was agreed on long before I was born. It's in balance, perfect balance. Everything as it should be. As you well know, Garfon."

"True," the man said. "And you know I've hardly ever used my powers either, Lemilla. I'm a good Gepethian, and proud of it."

"*Hardly* ever?" Lenora asked. This was interesting.

Garfon looked very sheepish. "Well, of course, I've made the occasional, uh, adjustment, now and then. Like, move a fly that's buzzing around my head over into the next field, make broccoli actually taste good, that sort of thing. Everybody does it all the time—and you can't tell me they don't, Lemilla, even if nobody ever wants to admit it. You do it too, Lemilla."

"Me? Move a fly?" The woman's face was white. "Honestly, Garfon. The very idea! And you! You ought to be ashamed of yourself. Calling yourself a good Gepethian! Honestly! Broccoli tastes just the way it should—perfect, and you know it!"

"Oh, I do, do I? So tell me, then, Lemilla, my dear wife—

what happened to that little scar you got on your cheek when that hot fat splashed up? Seems to me it was there just last week—and now—"

Lemilla blushed bright red and raised her hand to cover her unblemished cheek.

"Scar?" she said coldly. "What scar? I have no idea what you mean. None—why, I don't even know if I *have* any power."

Garfon snorted. Lenora decided to intervene before the argument became too serious.

"Of course you have power," she said. "Everyone in Gepeth does." That's certainly what her parents had always told her, and surely it was true. "But—do you mean to tell me that you work these fields and do all of that hard work with *no* help from your powers at all?" Lenora knew they weren't supposed to use their powers, of course. But was everybody in this country so obedient, so compliant? Was she the only one who refused to be "good"?

The husband and wife stopped glaring at each other and turned toward Lenora.

"Use our powers for work?" he said incredulously.

"Upset the Balance?" she objected.

"Good heavens," he added.

"What an idea," she said.

"*I* have powers," said a high-pitched voice at Lenora's elbow. It was Sayley, who had sidled up to Lenora in the midst of the conversation. "*And* I've used them. And not just on broccoli, either—although of course I do that, too. Broccoli is *so* awful, isn't it?" She paused and waited until Lenora nodded her agreement.

Then she continued. "But you know what, Leteshia? Why, one time, I even made the chairs talk! You should have heard what one said to my Aunt M—"

"Sayley," her mother interrupted. "That's enough. I don't ever want to hear about that chair incident again. I was *so* embarrassed, let me tell you. Your Aunt Mandrilen still hasn't forgiven me. And anyway—" her brow wrinkled—"you shouldn't be telling this young lady these things. Why, we hardly know her. And she's from the—well, you just shouldn't."

"Don't worry," Lenora said, "*I* don't mind—and I won't tell anyone. Why, I use *my* powers all the time."

"You do?" Sayley said, enthralled.

"You do?" repeated the adults, horrified.

"All the time," Lenora repeated firmly.

"But you shouldn't!" the woman said, her cheeks flushing. "I mean, the very idea. Think how boring life would be if all we had to do was imagine everything. You wouldn't work, there'd be no point. What would you do all day?"

"Have fun!" Lenora answered.

"Have fun!" echoed Sayley.

"Well, honestly!" She turned and gave Lenora a severe look. "Young lady, I'm afraid that you'll have to be on your way just as soon as this—whatever this is—goes away. I really can't have somebody with such dangerous ideas in my house. Think of the Balance! Think of the children!"

Lenora sighed. She was *very* good at getting in trouble.

"Well," she said, "if we Gepethians have agreed on everything, *this*—" she gestured at the melting white stuff still clinging to her shift "this stuff certainly isn't part of that agreement. So maybe we'll have to rethink everything—even if we don't want to."

"Nonsense," said the woman, anxiously. "It's some sort of—some sort of—thing. It'll go away. And everything will return to normal."

"I only wish I knew what it was," the man said.

"Oh, look!" said Sayley. The little girl had danced across the room and was looking out the window. "It's changing!"

Everyone in the room hurried to the window and crowded around as they tried to peer through the tiny panes.

The white stuff had stopped falling. In fact, the sky was blue, the sun was out, and, whatever the white material was, it seemed to be rapidly melting—turning into puddles of water, or at least something that looked a lot like water.

And Lenora was feeling quite warm now—as if the cold inside her were disappearing with the cold outside. It was time to go.

"I really can't thank you enough," she said, handing the woman her drink. "I'm sorry if I've annoyed you with my thoughts. If it hadn't been for you I could've died out there."

She peeked out the window again. Except for the melting white stuff piled here and there, it looked as if there had never *been* anything unusual.

"It was nothing," the man said. "Any good Gepethian would have done the same."

"We're only doing our part to keep the Balance," the woman added.

"Praise the Balance," they both said together.

"Praise the Balance," Lenora said, as she knew they expected her to—she'd already done more than enough to alarm them. "And I do thank you, and I won't disturb you any more. I'll be off now." She began to head for the door.

"May I come?" Sayley asked, tugging at Lenora's damp dress.

"No!" answered her mother and father together.

Lenora turned and smiled at her. "Better not. It's a long, hard journey. But it was lovely to meet you, Sayley." And she shook her hand.

Sayley looked very sad as she shook Lenora's hand. "Good-bye, then, Leteshia," she said. "Come back sometime?"

"I will if I can," said Lenora. And she headed through the door and out into the now balmy air and down the road again.

Giants, she thought. Discontent everywhere. And now this white stuff suddenly appearing out of nowhere and nearly freezing me to death—and just as suddenly disappearing again. Something is wrong. Something is very wrong.

8

Coren sat in a small arbor in the garden. He was hiding.

He didn't want to admit to himself that he was hiding. After all, he loved Lenora. Why wouldn't he want to see her? And hadn't he *wanted* her to settle down? To concentrate on their wedding? Then what was—

"Cori, dearest! There you are, you silly goose. I've been looking all over for you."

"Lenora!"

"No, no, it's Leni now, not Lenora. Lenora is so *stuffy!*"

She had changed dresses again. Now she was wearing some elaborate green and blue silk thing. Her hair was piled in a mass of curls on top of her head and her face looked—well, funny.

He looked more closely. "Lenora, is that—surely that isn't *paint* on your face?"

Lenora giggled.

"Not paint, silly. It's called makeup. Eyeliner, eye shadow, lip rouge, and cheek blusher! Aren't the names wonderful? And isn't it sweet? I don't know why I never wore it before."

"Because you look better without it?"

Lenora looked hurt, then smacked him lightly on the arm.

"Now *I* know you're just teasing me, sweetums, but another, more sensitive person might be hurt by a comment like that."

She did actually look hurt, too, under all that silly goop. Lenora, hurt by something he said! How strange.

"Anyway," she said, pulling him by the hand, "it's time to go. We have to hurry."

"Go? Where?"

"Back to Fullbright, of course. The darling man has come up with just the most gorgeous idea for the pew ribbons— you'll be so thrilled, Cori! See, it's lace and—no, I won't tell you! I want you to hear it from his very own lips. And we really have to start thinking about the choreography for the attendants during the ceremony."

Choreography? Was she totally out of her mind?

Well, italics were bad enough. There was no way he was going to sit around discussing choreography.

"I can't right now," Coren said, desperately, "I—I—I have to see Lufa. I promised her ages ago."

Lufa's name had just popped into his head, but, actually, going to see her was a good idea. The wise woman had been Lenora's friend and confidante for years. If anyone could help Coren to understand Lenora, it was Lufa.

"Lufa?" asked Lenora, wrinkling her nose. "Lufa is always *so* serious. And she never listens when I talk to her about important things. Like corsages, for instance—I wanted to choose flowers from her garden, and I did ask her ever so nicely, you know, and all she did was just nod and say she was too busy to worry about flowers and I could take whatever I wanted. Too busy to worry about flowers for an important occasion like a royal wedding—*my* wedding! Honestly, Cori, it just isn't natural! What do you have to see *her* about?"

"Well, uh—" Coren's mind raced. "Since I'm new to your country she has to teach me things, right? About your country," he added lamely. "She *is* the wise woman, after all."

Lenora didn't seem to find his excuse lame at all. "Good idea! You're going to need to know all the rules. We wouldn't want you embarrassing us during the ceremony by doing something wrong, would we? It might disturb the Balance, and that sweet, darling man, Agneth, would be *so* upset. Off you go then, Cori, dear, and come find me when you're finished. I'll be with Fullbright."

Coren nodded and trotted off, perplexed. This change in Lenora was all too swift and all too big. She was actually praising Agneth—and didn't seem to have much use for her best friend, Lufa. Yes, going to see Lufa wasn't such a bad idea after all.

As soon as he reached her small cottage near the woods, the door opened. He didn't even get a chance to knock.

"Come in," said the wise woman, taking him by the hand and pulling him through the door. "I've been expecting you."

"You have?"

"Oh, yes. I knew you'd be here, because I ran into Lenora earlier today. Something is very wrong with her."

Coren sighed in relief. "You noticed it, too? I'm so glad. I thought maybe it was just me."

Lufa showed him to a chair by the table. "She was actually choosing flowers, if you can imagine! But, Coren, I'm surprised at you. I would have thought this change would make you happy. She's so *sweet*. So *good*. So—"

"Dull," Coren muttered. He was so caught up in his thoughts that he hadn't even noticed the twinkle in the wise woman's eye.

"Dull?" Lufa teased. "Did I hear you right? Surely *you*,

Prince Coren of Andilla, didn't say that this new behavior of Lenora's is 'dull'? Or if you did, surely you meant it as a compliment? Didn't you always *want* Lenora to be dull?"

"Not *this* dull!" Coren objected. "And, anyway, I don't really want *her* to be dull. I just want our lives to be dull. Well, not dull, exactly, but a little more normal, you know, a little less filled with crazy adventures?"

"Is that so?" The expression on the wise woman's face changed, grew more serious. "But, Coren," she said, "surely those adventures came about as a result of her adventurous spirit? You can't lose one without the other, you know."

She was probably right. But it hardly mattered now, did it? Because Lenora *had* somehow lost her spirit of adventure—and he didn't like it.

"Do you think she's ill, Lufa?" he asked. "I mean, how could she change so quickly?"

Lufa shook her head. "I'm not sure. Actually, it concerns me a great deal. It seems as though—"

There was another knock at the door. A servant asked if Lufa would attend the king in the drawing room. Urgent business.

"Am I wanted, too?" Coren asked.

"You, sir?" The messenger looked as if he had no idea who Coren even was.

"You'd better come, too, Coren," Lufa said, giving him a comforting smile as she rose to her feet. "This might be important."

Yes, thought Coren to himself, too important for them to even think about me. But he went with her anyway.

As they hurried back along the path to the castle, the sky was clouding over, and a chill wind was blowing.

"That's strange," Lufa commented, "we aren't due for weather like this for months."

"Well," Coren commented, "you can't control the weather!"

And then he realized what he'd just said. He stopped dead. "But you do, don't you? It's always perfect here in Gepeth. Blue skies, hot in the afternoon, cool mornings and evenings. And it rains at least once a week, in fact now that I think about it, it rains every Sunday, doesn't it?"

"Between two and six," Lufa nodded. "Quite right. Into every life a little rain must fall—on schedule, as planned. Of course we control the weather. Generations ago this world of Gepeth was imagined a certain way and we uphold the tradition."

"The Balance," Coren nodded.

"Yes," Lufa said. "The Balance. And there's a good reason it's called that, too. Because it keeps everything *in* balance. Nobody always gets whatever they want, of course. But everyone gets as much as possible without depriving the rest of us. Like the rain, for instance—we all know we can't have picnics on Sunday afternoon, and we all accept it. It's a small price to pay for giving little children their weekly opportunity to splash in the puddles and making sure that the crops always get exactly the right amount of moisture at exactly the right time. And then we can always have our first fresh peas on May the fourth, Peasday—just as we do every year. Everyone accepts the Balance because it's the best arrangement for everybody."

"Lenora doesn't always accept it," Coren said. "Or, at least, she didn't used to always accept it. Now—"

"Now she's different—and," Lufa added as she shivered in the brisk wind, "she's not the only thing that's different, either."

As she wrapped her arms around herself, the wind grew even brisker. Leaves began blowing off the trees, and Coren had to concentrate on keeping his feet firmly on the ground. Suddenly the wind was so strong he could barely walk. It howled in his ears and he found himself growing frightened. The castle seemed very far away. Maybe they should take shelter in the nearest cottage. He started to yell this idea to Lufa when the wind literally knocked him off his feet and into the stone wall of the cottage.

Flattened against the wall, he saw laundry baskets, tree boughs, and small animals flying past in all directions, propelled by the wind, which was now so intense and so incredibly loud that its noise blotted out all other sounds.

What had happened to Lufa? He tried to inch his way along the wall, but the wind was too strong. He could hardly move at all. He sank to his knees, put his head down, and hoped nothing too large would happen to blow his way. Except for a wet apron from a clothesline, nothing did.

And then, just as suddenly as it began, the wind stopped. Everything fell from the air onto the ground beneath—including a tin kettle, which landed right on Coren's head with a large bang.

He staggered up, rubbing his head, and spotted Lufa. She was sitting against a tree trunk, half a watermelon on her head, the other half splattered over the rest of her.

He picked his way toward her through the blown and broken objects littered everywhere, then helped her get the watermelon off her head. Except for the watermelon juice that dribbled down her face, she seemed to be all right.

"Something is certainly out of balance," she said firmly. "Let's hurry, Coren." And she started toward the castle, picking watermelon seeds off her clothing as she went.

9

The strong castle walls had kept the wind out. Everything inside was as it was supposed to be.

Or, at least, almost everything. A fire blazed in the hearth—unheard of for a summer's afternoon. It must have been lit earlier, when the cold wind began. King Rayden paced in front of it, anxiously watched by a group of worried-looking councillors and by an even more worried Queen Savet, who was holding a piece of embroidery, just as usual, except that she wasn't making even an occasional stitch in it.

"Oh, Lufa," King Rayden said, as the wise woman and Coren came through the door. "We saw it all through the window—unbelievable! I'm glad you're not hurt. You aren't, are you?"

"I'm perfectly fine," said Lufa, glistening a little as the light of the fire reflected off the watermelon juice. "Coren is, too."

"Coren?" The king gave Coren a distracted glance, not even really seeing him. "Oh, good, good." Coren decided not to mention the large lump growing on his head.

"But," Lufa continued, "things are bad outside. As we made our way here we saw a lot of people who are disoriented and confused, and I'm afraid that some of the villagers have been quite seriously hurt." Her face tightened into an angry grimace. "I'd be surprised if there weren't a death or two."

"Deaths? Hurt? My villagers?" Queen Savet dropped her embroidery and rose to her feet. "We'll certainly have to do something about that. We'll open a temporary hospital—in the ballroom, I think. Yes, that would be best. The ballroom, Agorno—see to it."

One of the councillors bowed and rushed from the room.

"It'll have to be cleaned, of course, and disinfected." Still talking, Queen Savet headed over to the wall by the fire and grabbed the broom she insisted be kept there, awaiting just such an emergency as this. "Can't have sick people in a dusty ballroom. Let's see—beds, lamps, table, linens, blankets—and we'll need bandages and hot water. Kralno?"

"Yes, milady, I'll begin the arrangements." Another councillor hurried off.

"As for you, Lufa," she said, pointing the broom toward her, "we'll need the usual herbs and other medications. I hope you have plenty," she added grimly, glancing through the windows at the devastation outside.

Lufa nodded.

"And," Savet added, shouldering the broom, "I'll come with you, Lufa. I must go and comfort the relatives, and see to the—"

"Wait, Savet," Rayden said, sweat glistening on his forehead. "There's something Lufa has to hear first, and you might as well hear it, too. We've had some disturbing news. And—" his brow wrinkled— "and you know, I think this last awful business out there must relate to it somehow."

He gestured over to the wall by the door, where a young lad, no older than Coren, stood in muddy boots and farmer's work clothes, looking awed by his elegant surroundings.

"Listen to what this fellow has to say, Lufa. He's just now been brought up from the front gate. Come here, my lad, and tell your story again."

"But wipe your feet on that mat first," Queen Savet said, pointing to the floor in front of the door with her broom.

"Really, Savet," said Rayden. "How can you think of mud at a time like this? Speak, boy, speak."

But the boy had seen the look on Savet's face. As all the courtiers stared at him impatiently, he went to the mat and carefully wiped his boots, then moved gingerly forward over the royal carpets, a shy look on his face.

"Well, sir," he said, "it's like I told you. The morning started out normal like, and we were finishing breakfast, getting ready to go out to the fields—and then all this white stuff started to fall from the sky. Well, first the sky got all cloudy, *then* the white stuff fell. And the wind blew. And it got terribly cold—you wouldn't believe how cold. And if you held this white stuff in your hand it would melt, but if you went out in it, it surely started to freeze you up. It was like drowning in ice cream."

Lufa caught her breath. "Go on," she said.

He nodded and continued, so caught up in his story that he had forgotten to be nervous. "Well, then, after a few hours, it just went away. Like it never happened, you know. But my folks, Agarda and Podillo, they are, I don't suppose you know them? Well, they were pretty worried and thought you should know. So they sent me here, actually sent me, and none of us has ever been away from Bardno County before, you know, not even my father. It feels so strange. I didn't know the wind blew so strong in other places. There's no place like home, is there? But they said I had to come. Heaven knows what damage that white stuff's done to our crops."

"They're bound to be damaged," Lufa said. "It has that effect."

King Rayden turned to her. "You mean you know what it is?"

Lufa nodded. "Snow," she said.

"Snow?" Everyone in the room repeated the word. Including Queen Savet, who had been leaning on her broom and staring accusingly at the boy's still muddy boots.

"What is—snow?" Rayden asked.

"I know what snow is," said Agneth, the keeper of the Balance. He looked twice as worried as everyone else, and his thin face was white as a sheet. "Well," he went on, "that's to say, I don't actually know what it is. But I've seen the word before, in the old documents, in the Recordings of the keeper. It was something our ancestors felt was unnecessary to maintain the Balance." He turned to Lufa. "Come to think of it, it's forbidden, snow is. How did *you* know what it is?"

Lufa gazed at him coolly, a thin smile on her lips. "I *can* read, you know." She and Agneth had never been the best of friends. The keeper always worried over her experiments with herbs, and the fact that she kept books in the old languages and even knew how to read them.

"Oh," the councillor said. He looked a little flustered.

"And, in any case," Lufa added, "for something 'forbidden' and 'unnecessary,' it's doing a surprisingly good job of making its presence known. Like that tornado we just had."

"Tornado?" Rayden said.

"Also forbidden," Agneth said grimly. "So that was a tornado, was it? Interesting. I'd always thought of it as more like a large animal with a flexible spine. But my predecessors were right, no question about it. Such a thing is completely and absolutely unnecessary. Quite unbalanced."

"For once, Agneth," Lufa said, picking another watermelon

seed off her skirt, "I have to agree with you."

"Yes," said Rayden, his voice filled with worry. "How could those strange things appear just like that, without our consent?"

"And hurt my villagers," Savet added, vigorously shaking her broom back and forth. "I *must* see to them!"

"Soon, Savet. Soon," Rayden said. "The servants are there already, and I need you here. The more minds we have to think about all this, the better. There's also the matter of this giant."

"A giant," Agneth said. "Snow. A tornado. Monstrous aberrations! There's only one explanation. And we all know what it is."

"Yes," Rayden said, grimly. "Someone must have imagined them."

"Someone, indeed," said Agneth, eyebrows raised.

"I get your point, Keeper," Rayden said. He turned to the servant who waited by the door. "Bring Princess Lenora to me at once."

10

I think," Coren suddenly found himself saying, "that you'll find Lenora with Master Fullbright."

Well, everyone had forgotten he was even there—which was just fine with Coren. He didn't like attention—it always led to people expecting him to do things he didn't want to do. And he didn't mean to get Lenora into trouble, of course, but he had to speak. Agneth's logic was impeccable. She *was* the obvious explanation.

Rayden gave Coren a somewhat dazed look, then nodded at the servant, who hurried off. Then the king thanked the young farm lad for his information, rewarded him with some gold coins, and sent him on his way back home to Bardno.

As soon as he left, Queen Savet went over to where the boy had been standing and began to sweep vigorously at the carpet.

"Well," she said after a few moments of energetic sweeping, "that'll have to do for now. And I'm sorry, Rayden, but you'll just have to deal with that naughty girl without me. My people need me. Come as soon as you can, Lufa." She hurried out of the room before the king could stop her, sweeping the floor before her as she went.

The king watched her leave, an exasperated look on his face, then returned to his pacing. The councillors stood in small groups, whispering anxiously to one another. Coren could hear the words "tornado" and "Lenora" being used a lot, often in the same sentence.

Come to think of it, Coren told himself, they have a lot in common. Yes, the more he thought about it, the more suspicious of Lenora he was becoming.

"Someone sent for me?" Lenora said, brightly, as she entered the room.

The councillors turned as one and glared at her—and so did King Rayden. And Coren. There was a moment of awkward silence.

"What *have* you put on your face, Lenora?" Rayden finally said. "It looks dreadful!"

"It's called makeup, Father. Isn't that a cute name? I read about it in an old romance novel I found in the library, and I just had to imagine some for myself. I wasn't exactly sure what it looked like, of course—but this is how I imagined it and I know I must be right." Her voice grew small and wheedling, and she gave her father a shy look. "I hope you don't mind."

"Hmph," Agneth murmured. "Romance novels! I thought I'd burned all those dreadful things long ago. Talk about unbalance!"

"Anyway," Lenora continued, "you just think it's dreadful because you're not used to it, so I'll forgive you. Actually, it's exceedingly beautiful. It said so in the novel. And you know, Father, I believe that as a princess it's my duty to *set* the trends, not to follow them. Soon all the young ladies in Gepeth will be wearing it."

"Not if *I* have any say in the matter," Lufa growled.

"Nor I," Agneth added.

Everyone was furious with Lenora. Things were back to normal.

"Lenora," King Rayden said, "if you want to look like a clown, that's fine with me. Although I imagine Prince Coren will have something to say in the matter."

Oh, yes, Coren thought, I had something to say, all right—not that it made the slightest bit of difference.

"What I want," the king continued, "is an honest answer from you. Now tell the truth—did you create the tornado that just happened outside the castle grounds? Or the snow that fell in Bardno?"

"Tornado? Snow?" Lenora looked puzzled. "What are they, some kind of animals?"

Impatiently, Rayden explained.

"Good heavens," Lenora said, her eyes widening. "Those sound just too, too awful! They'd probably really muss up your hair and clothes, wouldn't they? And besides, imagining things like that upsets the Balance. I may create a little harmless makeup once in a while—but I'd never do an awful thing like that, Daddy."

"Daddy?" King Rayden repeated. He gave her a suspicious look. "Lenora, are you feeling all right?"

"Well, yes, Daddy, I am. But I do have an *awful* lot on my mind right now. I have to finish these wedding plans and then Coren and I are to go to the Islands, on an actual journey, and—"

"What about the giant?" King Rayden asked.

"Giant? Oh, you mean that big ugly monster in the North. Gosh, I'd completely forgotten about him—there *is* so much to think about. Why, we haven't even begun on the choreography! Anyway, Daddy, I'm sure you and your people will take care of him. I'm *far* too busy!"

Everyone stared at Lenora in disbelief.

"May I go now, Daddy?" she said impatiently. "Fullbright is waiting."

King Rayden nodded, and Lenora hurried from the room.

Rayden looked at Agneth. "Maybe my saying 'no' to her about the giant upset her so much that her poor little mind snapped."

Agneth snorted. "Not likely. No, Rayden, she was toying with you, couldn't you tell? She was acting."

Coren felt a nudge in his ribs. It was Lufa, giving him a look that clearly meant she wanted him to tell the king about his experiences with Lenora.

"Uh, I don't think Lenora is pretending," he said, in a surprisingly loud voice.

Everyone turned and stared at him, until he felt quite intimidated.

"Explain why, Coren," Lufa said, encouraging him.

"Well, because she's been behaving that way for hours now. She's been behaving strangely ever since she found out she couldn't go after the giant."

"I can confirm that," Lufa said. "There is definitely something wrong with her."

"And—" Coren hesitated, "and there's more. I entered her mind." He paused and blushed. He knew how they all hated the idea that he could just wander in and out of their heads anytime he pleased. "I only did it because I was so concerned," he pleaded. "She was acting so strangely, and—and—well, anyway, there was nothing there."

"Nothing?" Lufa said. "What do you mean, nothing?"

"I mean just that. Nothing. Nothing at all. Nothing except wedding plans and happiness."

Agneth came over and glared into Coren's eyes. "This *is* the Princess Lenora you're talking about?" Coren gulped, and nodded.

"Wedding plans?" Lufa said.

King Rayden shook his head. "And happiness. This is bad, very bad. As if a giant weren't bad enough, there's snow, *and* a tornado—and now Lenora has become happy. And we have to get the village cleaned up, and meanwhile that giant is still out there causing trouble in the North. I don't know what to do first."

"Deal with the giant," Agneth said decisively. "The other things have gone away, for now at least. But as far as we know, the giant is still there. We can't have a mammoth irregularity like that loose in the land."

"I agree," said Lufa. "And Savet seems to have the rescue operation well in hand, so you don't have to worry about that."

"Well, then," Rayden said, "we'll proceed as planned. I'll gather the thinking party here and we'll see if we can imagine that giant away. I'll need you, Lufa. And—good heavens, Prince Coren, are you still here?"

"Uh, yes, sir."

"Well, of course, we won't need you for the giant, will we, my lad? Not with your, uh, little handicap. How about going off to see if you can sort out what is the matter with Lenora?"

"Yes, sir," Coren agreed, trying to hide his fury at the king's suggestion that he was of no use. Just because he came of a different people with different powers didn't mean he was handicapped. It was the Gepethians who were handicapped. Why, he could think of a hundred different ways his own powers might be useful in this situation.

Not that he was about to suggest any of them to Rayden. Handicapped, indeed. How insulting! Let him try to do it his own way.

Coren left the drawing room in a huff and headed off to find Lenora.

11

He had almost reached Fullbright's quarters in the east wing when, suddenly, his father's image filled his mind.

"Father!" Coren was surprised. He hadn't had mental communications with his parents since they'd returned home to Andilla some weeks earlier. They knew how much he disliked using his powers, and he'd assumed they'd finally accepted it and begun to treat him as a Gepethian.

Like a person with a handicap.

"Hello, Coren, my lad!" King Arno's words echoed in his mind. It felt surprisingly good. He hadn't experienced anyone doing that for such a long time.

"What are you doing here, Father? And how is everything in Andilla?"

A troubled look passed over the face in Coren's mind.

"Well, my boy," Arno said, "that's what I'm here to tell you. I hate to trouble you, just before the wedding. We were making plans to come back there to Gepeth when—when—"

As he talked, his face began to fade out a little, and then it returned.

"There it goes again," the king said.

"There goes what?" Coren asked.

"Everything," Arno said. "That's the whole trouble."

"I don't understand."

"Here," Arno said impatiently. "Let me show you."

A series of pictures passed through Coren's mind. It was Andilla. But it wasn't Andilla as Coren remembered it.

First, Coren saw the royal ballroom as his father usually thought of it—the rich mahogany panels gleaming, the comfortable padded chairs upholstered in colorful plaids, the bearskins on the floor, the hunting trophies and weapons hanging on the walls.

Then he saw the same room as he knew his mother usually thought of it—she'd shown it to him often enough in her efforts to get him to appreciate the pleasures of the mind. It was a bewildering kaleidoscope of many colors, always shifting from one to another. The chairs all looked like fluffy white clouds floating some distance above the mirrorlike floor and hummed beautiful melodies in unison with one another.

Well, there was certainly nothing unusual in any of that. Coren was only seeing what his parents usually imagined.

But then the image shifted again, and Coren saw the *actual* ballroom—the one he himself had resolved to be content with when he'd decided not to use his powers of thought. There were ancient, blue brocade draperies hanging in tatters and covered with dust, broken windowpanes in the high, arched windows—and the bent and broken chairs were old and dust covered and had stuffing and springs emerging from the many holes in their surfaces.

Strange that his father would want to show him that—or even know it was there. Arno never let his mind see the way things actually were if he could possibly help it—nor did anyone else in Andilla. Which was why the furniture was so dilapidated and the room was so filthy. Why bother fixing or cleaning if you could just think of things being any way you wanted them? Coren had always believed that Arno had never once in his life actually seen the real ballroom—yet now here it was, in his father's mind.

Then the image shifted again. Some of the torn brocade still remained, but some was replaced by his mother's shifting kaleidoscope of shimmering rainbows, and some was replaced by his father's cheerful curtains of plaid, the occasional animal head emerging between them. Clouds floated over the torn sofas and in between the plaid-covered chairs. As Coren watched, one of the clouds became a fluffy bearskin rug.

"Good heavens, Father," Coren said. "What does it all mean?"

"We don't know," said King Rayden, his face once more replacing the ballroom scene in Coren's head. "It just keeps on happening. You see, Coren, our imaginings are flickering."

As if to show what he meant, King Arno's face suddenly flickered-to be replaced by the head of a goat wearing a jewel-encrusted gold crown.

"Now where did *that* come from?" Arno said wearily as his own face returned. "It's happening all the time now, Coren. One minute we imagine we're lying on a soft bed covered with a goose-down quilt, the next minute we're lying on a lumpy mattress covered with a rough wool blanket."

That's the trouble with living in your mind, Coren thought. Nothing is real.

"Never mind the lectures," Arno snapped.

Oops. Coren was so unused to using his powers he'd forgotten that Arno would overhear him.

"We're in serious trouble, Coren," the king continued.

"Something is affecting our powers. All our imaginings are flickering, all our thoughts are getting mixed up with one another, and you have to add no more than half a cup of brown sugar if you want it to come out crispy and crunchy. Bother! It just happened again. I'd better hurry up, Coren—who knows when we're going to get cut off, or whether I'll even be able to speak to you again. Listen, Coren, and listen carefully."

"Yes, Father, I'm listening."

"Good." A white cook's hat now appeared on the king's head. "Bake in a 350 degree oven for half an hour, or until it's just lightly browned."

Not even pausing for a moment, the king pulled off the hat and threw it over his shoulder. "I want you to go to King Rayden and find out if anything odd is happening there in Gepeth, too."

"But, Father," Coren said, "something odd *is* happening here." And quickly he related to his father all the latest events— or at least as many as he could actually manage to communicate in the circumstances. At one point his father turned into a talking dandelion plant, fluffy seeds flying from his hair as he nodded at Coren's story. At another point he simply disappeared altogether. And even when Coren saw his father's own face in his mind, Arno continually interrupted Coren's story with advice about baking buns. By the time he finished telling Arno about recent events in Gepeth, Coren was really worried.

"So it's happening in both our countries," Coren said. "Things are out of control."

"Arno! Arno!" It was Coren's mother, and she sounded very, very frightened. "Come quickly!"

Coren now saw his mother and, behind her, the image of a magnificent castle crumbling into a dilapidated old ruin.

"Must go, son," Arno said quickly. "Talk to you soon—I hope."

And then he was gone.

"Ah, Cori! There you are!" This time the voice was coming through his ears, not from inside his head. He turned to see Lenora standing behind him.

"Now *do* hurry," she said, grabbing his hand and beginning to pull him down the corridor. "Because Fullbright and I can't make any more important decisions until we decide on a basic color scheme. He wants blue and green, the old dear—and I see his point, of course. But I do so love pink, don't you? Pink and white. Pink and white, or blue and green. Which one do you like, Cori?"

"Neither," he snapped. "Don't you think, Lenora, that there are more important things to worry about? Didn't you even notice that tornado? And now I've been hearing that things are happening in Andilla, too, and—"

She came to a full stop, dropped his hand, and glared at him.

"I already told you," she said, very annoyed, "I don't have time for all that! Let Father deal with it. It's his job, not mine. Honestly. When you're in a better humor you can come and speak to me. Until then, go be cranky somewhere else." And she flounced off down the corridor.

Coren stood there bewildered and *very* worried. Giants, tornados, snow, trouble in Andilla—and Lenora not at all herself. What was happening?

12

Lenora walked down the road feeling very unsettled. In the fields around her were farmers inspecting the damage, so upset that they weren't even singing their jolly songs. That was one good thing at least. Still, it was hard not to be distressed by all the devastation—particularly when the fields contained so many dead animals, cows and sheep and pigs, apparently killed somehow by the white substance.

The air was moist, like after a heavy rain, and steam rose from the wet ground as the hot sun evaporated the water. Lenora certainly wasn't cold anymore. In fact, her clothes were beginning to stick to her in the heat. She stopped to wipe the sweat from her eyes.

As she did, the road changed. It just suddenly became a different road. It was no longer the rough gravel trail she'd been traveling ever since she left home. Now it was wide and smooth and deep black—and for some peculiar reason, it had a yellow line right down the middle. What could *that* possibly be for? Although, Lenora thought, it was rather attractive—different. It was an unusual idea, decorating roadways.

Also, she quickly discovered, it was very easy to walk on the smooth black surface. No lumps beneath your feet. She rather liked it.

The yellow line and the smooth black surface ended as abruptly as they had started, so that Lenora stumbled and nearly fell. The road was back to gravel again.

The really odd thing was, Lenora could have sworn that she'd followed that interesting yellow line with her eyes way off into the distance—as far down the road as she could see. And now, it wasn't there at all—and when she turned and looked back, it wasn't there, either. It and the black smooth surface had disappeared altogether.

Well, this really *was* strange. It was obvious that somebody was reimagining things. But who, and why?

Well, whoever it was, Lenora didn't like it. All those poor dead animals—it was cruel. In fact, she was beginning to wonder about this whole adventure. The faster she got to that giant and settled the entire matter, the better.

As much as she hated to admit it, Lenora was a little frightened. She was actually thinking how nice it would be to be back home, being reassured and comforted by her parents—and by Coren.

Yes, she told herself, why not just try to imagine myself where the giant is, right now? My mental images of the north counties are a little fuzzy. But if I try really hard, it will probably work. It *has* to work.

Before she could even begin to try, she was distracted by a shout behind her.

"Leteshia! Wait for me!"

It was Sayley, the little girl from the cottage, galloping up on a huge and very impressive-looking mare.

"Whoa!" Sayley called out, as she pulled the horse to a

sudden stop only inches from Lenora and then patted it and said, "good horsie."

"Sayley! What are you doing here?"

The little girl set her lips in a determined way. "I snuck out," she said defiantly. "They said I couldn't come with you, and they even locked me up in my room, just because I had a little bit of a tantrum! I hardly even screamed at all. But they couldn't stop *me*! I waited until they all went out in the fields, and then I imagined this mare, and here I am!" She stopped and giggled. "You should see the mess the mare made of my bedroom!"

This was terrible—how could Lenora deal with the giant and everything with a child to look after? Particularly a child as willful as this one—*and* her parents would be furious. And very worried.

"Sayley, you can't come with me. It's too dangerous, and—"

But as Lenora spoke, she could see the storm growing in Sayley's eyes.

"I want to come!" she wailed. "I want to come, and I will, I will, I w—"

Her words were cut off as her face filled with fear. The mare had suddenly begun to rear uncontrollably, neighing in terror, her eyes rolling back.

The road had changed again, right under Lenora's feet—and the mare's hooves. And now, zooming rapidly toward them over the smooth black surface were three shiny black machines that looked rather like giant dragonflies without the wings—like something out of her fantasy books, Lenora thought. The machines were making an incredibly loud noise, enough almost to deafen her.

As the machines came closer, the noise turned into a high-pitched squeal. And then the noise cut off as the machines stopped, just a few feet in front of Lenora. Sayley was having real trouble controlling the mare, and Lenora gripped its reins to try to help her. Finally, when the mare did calm down a bit, she turned to get a closer look at what had disturbed it.

The machines were some kind of vehicle, apparently—because now she could see that a person sat atop each one.

There were three men. Two of them were hugely overweight, and as if to make it worse, they were wearing tight blue pants, not at all becoming on men so heavy. One of them wore a sleeveless leather jacket that revealed strange pictures covering his arms. Lenora wasn't close enough to make out what they were, but they looked quite revolting—all black and blue and red, like bruises.

The third man, the one in front, was tall and skinny, with a scraggy beard and the same blue pants, except his had huge holes in the knees. Had he never heard of a thread and needle? If Lenora's mother ever saw pants like that, she'd have a conniption.

"Victims," the skinny one said. "At last." He glared at them menacingly as a nasty smile spread over his ugly face.

Lenora glared right back. No one talked to her that way.

The skinny one just kept smiling and then lifted his hand and pointed something toward Sayley. "You, kid," he growled. "You up there on the animal. Get off, right now—or I'll make you get off."

By now all three of the men were pointing those things at them. Lenora decided that they had to be weapons. But she couldn't imagine what harm they could do. They weren't even sharp. Nothing but metal tubes with handles. Maybe you blew into the other end, like a peashooter.

Fancy-looking peashooters, indeed. Just who did they think they were dealing with? Just as she was about to tell them how silly they were being, Sayley spoke

"I will not get off this animal," she said, in a chillingly determined voice. "Not unless *I* choose to—and I don't choose to. Now go away."

Well, Lenora thought, you had to hand it to her—the child didn't lack for courage. These men were silly, maybe, but they did seem to imagine they were pretty scary. And Sayley wasn't scared at all. Maybe having her around wasn't such a bad idea after all.

"Yes," added Lenora, "do go away, before we're forced to do something about it. And stop waving those silly peashooter things at us."

"Shut up," the skinny one growled, his eyes narrowing. "We want your money, lady. Now."

"Too bad," Lenora replied. "You can't have it."

"No," Sayley added, "you can't, so there. What's money, Leteshia?"

Lenora didn't know and was too busy thinking up a weapon to bother answering. A giant peashooter of her own would do the trick. One with balls of honey inside instead of peas—she didn't really want to hurt them, after all, just make them a little uncomfortable and show them how silly they were being.

She began to move toward them, the idea for the weapon forming in her brain.

POW! A horrible noise rang out, and the beautiful mare screamed in terror, then sank to its knees, nearly pushing Lenora over. Sayley was able to leap off just in time to avoid being crushed herself, then rushed into Lenora's arms, shivering and sniffling, clearly terrified.

"Wh-what happened, Leteshia? My mare—it—they—" Her words broke off in a distressed sobbing. For all her courage, she really was only a child—and these bullies didn't even care.

As Lenora hugged the child and tried to comfort her, she looked in horror at the blood pouring from the mare's chest. The mare's eyes glazed over, she fell onto her side, she shook violently a few times. Then she was still.

For a moment Lenora was speechless. Sayley's beautiful horse, dead. Wounded in some strange way by that loud noise. Where had it come from?

Those men—those bullies. They had done something. Lenora turned and looked at the weapons they were holding with a new respect.

This could never happen in Gepeth. No Gepethian would ever hurt an animal in this way. Therefore these men were not from Gepeth. They didn't belong here.

She tried to disappear them. Nothing. Nothing happened at all.

One of them got off his vehicle, sneering, and began to move toward them, still pointing his dangerous peashooter in their direction. Sayley's sobs turned into frightened gasps as she shivered uncontrollably in Lenora's arms. Lenora tried once more to imagine a weapon for herself—but still nothing happened.

No powers. Again. Were she and Sayley going to end up like the mare?

And then, suddenly, the men were gone, disappeared completely. And the road was gravel again.

But the mare was still dead. As Lenora looked at it lying there on the gravel, the blood still wet, she felt horrible. And Sayley probably felt even worse. She had imagined this beautiful creature into existence, and now it was dead.

Sayley was whimpering, staring at the dead horse. Lenora hugged her more closely.

"I—I'm scared, Leteshia. I want to go home. Right now!"

Lenora suddenly found herself hugging nothing but air. Her arms were empty. Sayley was gone.

Poor child—she must have imagined herself home without even realizing she was doing it. She had an amazingly powerful mind, for a child. Lenora hoped her parents wouldn't be too hard on the poor little thing. She'd learned her lesson already, the hard way.

Sayley was gone, but the horse was still there. It made Lenora feel very uncomfortable. A creature as beautiful as that, filled with life one moment and the next moment—Lenora could hardly bring herself to look at it.

What should she do? Should she try to imagine it alive again and without the wound?

But, no, she couldn't do that, it seemed wrong, somehow. Let the horse die in peace, in good Gepethian style.

But the mare was certainly too big to bury, the way her father buried his horses when they became old and died. Lenora had no choice but to try to imagine it away for good. It wasn't a respectful act, of course, and it wouldn't be something she would ever be proud of. But it was better than leaving the poor animal dead there on the road.

But would her powers work now? Well, Sayley's had, enough to drag her back home as soon as she wanted to be there. So maybe—

Lenora closed her eyes and imagined the mare gone. When she opened them again, the horse *was* gone. Thank goodness.

But the blood remained on the road.

Lenora stood there for some time, looking at the blood. Then she shook her head and tried to pull herself together.

Where had those horrible men come from? How could they harm a beautiful creature like the mare? Why wouldn't her powers work when they were here?

If this *was* the work of some uncontrolled mind, she didn't like the mind. If it wasn't—then what was it?

And things were getting worse all the time. Something had to be done, and soon.

Maybe, somehow, it was tied into the giant. Hadn't it all started when it appeared? Yes, maybe that was it.

But where had the giant come from? Well, it didn't matter—it had to be got rid of. It made no sense, but Lenora found herself thinking that getting rid of the giant would somehow make up for the loss of the mare. And after she got rid of it, she could just wish herself home, the way Sayley had—and hope that her parents wouldn't be too hard on her, either.

Yes, she told herself ruefully, I seem to be learning *my* lesson the hard way, too—just like Sayley.

She closed her eyes and tried to recapture an image of the north counties from the mists of her memory. What she saw was pretty foggy. It was a gamble, all right, jumping into something so uncertain. She might find herself in a half-formed world. And before she jumped, she'd certainly have to try to erase the words hanging over the heads of the sheep—the ones that had identified what breeds they were in that picture in her geography book. If she didn't, she'd find herself in a country of the imagination where gigantic words like Kitznoldian Curlyroot and Domestic Cross floated forbiddingly overhead all the time. Not the real north counties at all.

But she had to chance it. She had to get there. She sighed and closed her eyes and imagined herself beside one of the sheep.

13

When Lenora opened her eyes, she found herself in a craggy but beautiful place. There were high hills with mountains in the distance, outcroppings of rock, heather, and brisk winds that didn't feel all that summery to Lenora. She imagined herself into a warm jacket and was about to head off down the hill to see if she'd come to the right place when she heard an astonishingly loud noise coming from the rocky crag behind her.

"FOOD!" it said. "YUM!"

Suddenly, something descended from above, as if out of the heavens. A hand, a huge leathery hand, about twice as tall as Lenora herself. The hand encircled and engulfed a sheep that had been grazing nearby, no more than a few meters away from where Lenora stood. The sheep was, Lenora guessed, a Kitznoldian Curlyroot. You could tell, she vaguely remembered, by the crinkly wool.

The hand went upward again toward an astonishingly huge face that had popped up over the rocky crag and hovered in the sky above her, like a giant sun. The huge hand went toward the huge mouth and then came away again, sheep still in it.

"UGH! UGHY WUGHY!" The sheep was placed back on

the ground, bleating and rather wet, and then the hand moved over to a Mazerian nut tree that stood nearby, pulled it out of the ground, roots and all, and stuffed it into the mouth instead. Lenora heard a terrifying crunching sound, then saw what seemed to be the roots shoot out of the giant's mouth and hit the hill, not far from her.

"YUM!" declared the giant. "MORE!" And then the huge face looked back behind it in the other direction and disappeared down behind the rocky hill.

It was the giant she had come to find. This was the real North, all right.

The good thing was, the giant hadn't even noticed her standing there. Too busy thinking about food, she guessed.

The bad thing was that it was there at all—and thinking about food. When she'd pictured the giant she hadn't realized how big it had to be. Or how scary. That huge mouth, that huge, thunderous voice.

Lenora, Princess of Gepeth, actually shivered for a moment. The giant had to be got rid of, and the sooner the better. She wanted to simply turn and run. But she forced herself to head forward, toward the shrieks of "FOOD! FOOD!"

As she reached the top of the hill and looked over into the next valley, she gasped. She could see destruction everywhere. In the village nestled below, entire houses were smashed, fences knocked over, trees snapped. Farther off in the distance, on the other side of the village, Lenora could see the giant himself, towering over the countryside, creating huge pits as he walked, occasionally reaching down and grabbing a nut tree or entire clumps of berry bushes and stuffing them into his mouth.

There was no time to delay. Lenora immediately focused all of her mental energy outward, onto the figure of the giant across the valley. Then she willed the giant out of existence—threw it away.

But it didn't go away. It was still there. She tried again. Nothing. No powers—just like before.

As Lenora stood fuming, the giant turned around and began to head back toward her, flattening a farmhouse as he walked. Lenora hoped that the residents had fled already and that the farmhouse was empty. In the circumstances, it would certainly have been the sensible thing to do.

It was obviously the sensible thing for Lenora to do herself—just go, and as fast as she could. Be elsewhere. Unfortunately, she quickly discovered that her powers had stopped working altogether. She tried to imagine herself home. Nothing! It appeared that she was stuck here—and the giant was coming closer all the time.

As Lenora watched, she realized how very much she didn't like the feelings she was having. She wasn't even sure what to call them—it was like nothing she'd ever felt before. She imagined it was the way little babies must feel when they cry and no one comes. She searched for a word in her mind.

Helpless. That was the word. She felt helpless. And she hated it. It was almost unbearable to have things happen to you and not be able to change anything. It was the very worst thing imaginable, to have your ideas and your wishes just exist inside your head. Surely no human being could possibly live like that for long and not go completely mad.

Now the giant was bending over again—and plucking something small and pink out of the window of a house. It was a tiny child—a helpless human child. Oh, no, surely the giant wasn't going to—

Lenora watched in tense horror as the giant brought the

tiny pink figure up to his face, then, as the child's arms and legs wriggled in the air, held it pinched between two fingers and peered at it for what seemed like hours. Finally, the giant's hand dropped to the ground again and let the child go. Apparently, it wasn't a human child that the giant was hungry for—at least not right at that moment. Thank goodness for that. The giant watched as the child scurried away from it and hid in a corn-field. Then it headed onward, thoughtlessly kicking over the child's home as it went.

And she was just as helpless as that poor frightened child. She found herself thinking about Coren—wishing that he were there with her, hugging her, comforting her, giving her the strength to go on.

Not, she reminded herself, that Coren would be much help in a situation like this. He'd take one look at that giant below—which now, for some reason, seemed to be standing on its hands, waving its huge feet back and forth just beneath the clouds, and crowing wildly—Coren would take one look, and he'd turn into a quivering mass of jelly. He'd just be one more problem to add to all the others.

In midcrow, the giant lost its balance, teetered, and fell with a huge thump, then shrieked as the pointed tip of a church spire punctured the massive leather jerkin covering his stomach. The giant grabbed the spire, now broken off from the crushed church, pulled it from where it had stuck in the leather, and angrily threw it away. It landed with a huge crash in what was left of a barn that was already severely tromped.

Lenora winced at the tremendous racket. She had never felt so alone. Oh, if only Coren *were* here—and, somehow, not afraid. Here, but without all his worries and concerns. That's what she needed—Coren, smart and thoughtful and comforting and lovable as always, but also full of adventurous spirit, ready to reassure her and help her face that gruesome giant. Yes, she could just see him striding up the hill behind her, his adorable high cheekbones and full mouth moving closer all the time, his red hair and his freckles shining in the sunlight, his eyes gleaming fire, and a sword in his hand, saying, "Let's go! That giant won't wait for us! Come on, Lenora. Let's get him, right now!"

As she heard those comforting words echo in her mind, she felt something grabbing onto her arm, pulling her backward, and almost toppling her. She turned in fury to find out who or what had dared to do it—and stopped dead.

It was him! Coren! She wasn't imagining after all! Coren was there, really there, just when she most needed him!

But he had a sword in his hand! Coren was actually holding a sword! And he was waving it about impatiently. And he was dressed in armor, of all things! A complete suit of armor, gleaming brightly in the sun!

"But—but why are you here? And how did you get here?"

"Never mind that," Coren declared. "I'm here. And we have to go, right now. Do you know where the giant is?"

"Over there, somewhere," said Lenora, waving vaguely over her shoulder in the direction of the valley below. "Is that sword real?"

"Of course it's real," Coren exploded. "I'm going to slay this giant! Now, let's go, Lenora."

Lenora was confused, to say the least. This was all so unlike Coren!

"It's not unlike me at all, Lenora," he declared. "You've just never seen this part of me before."

And now he was reading her mind! He knew she hated that!

"You just hold on a minute, Coren," she began, but she didn't get a chance to finish.

He stamped his foot impatiently. "You don't seem to be getting it, Lenora. There's a giant out there—a dangerous giant. No time for lectures. And, anyway, you can stop thinking that, because you couldn't punch me in the stomach even if you tried. I wouldn't let you—and this magnificent, top-quality armor would protect me even if you did. And I'm surprised, a princess like you having such unladylike thoughts. Now, let's go!" And before she even knew what was happening, he had grabbed her wrist once more and was dragging her down the hillside, shouting "At it! At it! At it!" as he wildly waved the sword in front of him, his armor clanking loudly with every step.

Lenora was steaming mad. How *dare* he? Show up here wearing a noisy tin can and start ordering her about. How dare he, Coren, of all people, order her about?

But there didn't seem to be anything she could do about it. He was pulling her so fast that it took all her effort to stop herself from tumbling down the hill. And now she could see a horse that was tied to a tree at the foot of the hill. It was a magnificent animal, a huge white charger a good deal taller and larger and fiercer looking than the unusually sizable mare Sayley had created. Huge saddlebags hung from its jewel-encrusted saddle, filled with objects that created oddly shaped lumps in their sides, and with long, sharply pointed lances sticking out of them.

Lenora couldn't have imagined a better horse herself. Where had Coren got it?

As Coren pulled Lenora toward it, the horse reared and whinnied. "Stop that, Gruffo, right now," Coren ordered in a masterful voice. The horse immediately calmed down. Then Coren put a hand on the pommel of the saddle and leaped up onto the horse, his other hand still waving the sword.

"Come on, Lenora," he shouted down at her. "Hop on! You can't do much to help, I guess, because, after all, you're just a girl, right? But at least you can come and watch me destroy that measly giant. Hurry up, or I'll go without you!" He removed his hand from the pommel and thrust it down toward her.

Just a girl, indeed! She was so furious with him she wanted to reach up and grab the metal-clad fingers waving in front of her face and pull the conceited blowhard right off the horse and then give him a kick where it would hurt the most.

Of course, with all that dumb armor, she'd hurt her foot more than she'd hurt him. And then he'd probably just ride off without her.

She couldn't stand the thought of being left up here on the hilltop to watch as the foolhardy ninny rode straight toward the waiting jaws of the giant and inevitable doom. He *was* Coren after all, even if he was acting strangely.

With a sigh, she grabbed onto his hand, and with what appeared to be a surprisingly small amount of effort, Coren pulled her up onto the horse behind him.

"Gee-up, Gruffo!" he shouted, and off they rode, up and over the brow of the hill and then down into the valley below, Lenora holding onto Coren with both arms, Coren wildly brandishing the sword as he shouted "At it! At it!" in a gleeful voice.

It was the last straw. "I wish you'd put that silly thing away," she yelled into his ear. "We need to use our brains, Coren—and our powers, if they'll actually work for once. That silly sword will seem like a little needle to this giant."

"My magnificent sword? A needle? Hah!" he said, thrusting it outward. "Don't forget, it's merely a giant—and I am Coren! Coren the Bold of Andilla!"

What had gotten into him?

And wasn't it odd that he'd appeared just as she'd been thinking of him? A little too odd?

And then it hit her. Could she have created a new Coren for herself—just as earlier she'd thought up a second Lenora?

She thought back. She *had* been wishing for him. Wishing for Coren, but without all his annoying habits. Wishing for a Coren who wouldn't be afraid. Who would be brave enough to calm her and help her with the giant. And—here he was!

But she'd just been wishing, daydreaming. She hadn't meant to—

But apparently it had happened anyway. It was the only logical explanation. She had created another Coren. Her heart sank. Her powers didn't work when she needed them to, and when she didn't want them to work, they did!

She needed to talk to him, to see if her theory was right. "Coren!" she called. "Stop the horse!"

"No time," he shouted. "Got to get that giant. And you know, Lenora, the name Coren is so, so, I don't know, so dull! Call me—Cori! Yes. Cori. At it! At it!"

This was the limit. Impatiently, Lenora reached around him, his armor digging uncomfortably, and grabbed at the reins. "Whoa!" she called out. The horse stopped so quickly it nearly pitched both of them off.

"Just what do you think you're doing?" he shrieked, trying to grab the reins from her hands.

"Now you listen here, Coren," she said, holding on as tightly as she could.

"Cori," he interrupted, pulling remorselessly on the reins, which were now digging into her palm in a very painful way. "Cori."

"*Coren*," she repeated. "How did you get here?"

"How? Well, I—I don't know," he said impatiently, turning toward her. "What does it matter? I'm here and there's a giant to slay. And you're being a terrible nuisance, Lenora. Just like a woman, eh? Now give me those reins!" With a sudden wrench, he pulled the reins out of her hand and called out "Forward, Gruffo!" With a jolt, the horse began moving again.

"Ooh!" she exclaimed, as she grabbed onto Coren's neck to stop herself from falling off. "Impossible."

Maybe I should make him disappear, Lenora thought, as she bumped up and down on the hard saddle and watched the damaged streets of the devastated village pass by in a confused blur. After all, he's just an accident, a case of wishful thinking, my powers out of wack. After all, things, *people*, shouldn't just appear because you *think* about them. Usually she could control her thoughts. She kept her daydreams daydreams, and only the things she *wanted* to appear ever actually appeared.

Well, unless you counted the entire world she'd created with Hevak as leader. That *had* been a bit of an accident.

Anyway, she'd have to get rid of this extra Coren.

But how could she, now that he was actually here? He was alive, wasn't he? Like Sayley's mare. Could she simply blot him out, extinguish him?

They were through the village already, and the horse was pounding along a narrow road, getting closer to the giant with every hoofbeat.

Oh, what a mess!

14

"W hoa!" Coren shouted—and just in time. Dead ahead, only a few meters down the road, something very big and brown had suddenly descended. They'd almost plowed right into it.

As Lenora looked at it more closely she realized it was a shoe—a giant shoe, with a giant foot inside, and a giant leg emerging upward from its top.

It was the giant. His massive body loomed over everything.

"Ha, ha!" yelled Coren. "Here he is! Finally! I'll finish him! I'll slay him! Death to all giants!" He waved his sword in the air, screaming, "At it, at it, at it!"

"Shut up, Coren," she whispered, clutching at his arm, "don't make him mad." She glanced up to see how the giant was responding to all this. So far, apparently, he hadn't even noticed them—he seemed to be staring at something off in the distance.

"Really, Lenora," Coren said in a withering voice. "'Shut up' is a *very* rude thing to say. And you a princess! Do try to mind your manners."

"Mind my manners?" Lenora repeated. She was completely flabbergasted. He was sitting there waving a stupid weapon and telling *her* to mind her manners? Maybe she'd better disappear him after all—before this thing got out of hand. After all, really, he was just a figment of her imagination, and any minute the giant might notice them. Then what?

Well, she was sorry, but *both* the giant and the Coren would have to go.

First things first, though—she'd never be able to concentrate on unimagining the giant with that awful ruckus this Coren insisted on making.

"Mind my manners, indeed," she said. "You aren't really Coren, you know. I made you up, and now I'm going to unmake you." And she willed the Coren away.

"Hey," he objected. "Stop! That tickles!"

But she didn't stop. She kept right on willing.

Coren squirmed and wiggled for a while. But, in the end, he was still sitting there on the saddle in front of her.

"I know what you were trying to do," he said. "I *can* read minds, after all. What a horrible thing! Anyway, I *am* Coren, and you know it. And there's work to be done!" He thrust his sword upward toward the giant again. "At it! At it! At it!" he shouted. "Gee-up, Gruffo!"

As the horse began to move again, Lenora sighed. It seemed as if this Coren wasn't going anywhere—except forward toward his certain doom and hers. Better work on the giant, before he decided to lift his foot and stomp them both to mush. The Coren wouldn't think *that* tickled.

As the horse galloped ever closer, Lenora stared up at the giant's face and carefully and completely willed him away.

"WHO'S THAT THERE?" a giant voice boomed. "THEREDY WEREDY WHERE?" He'd noticed them now. He was looking down at them.

She willed some more.

"WHO ARE YOU?" the giant said. "TALK TO ME! TALKIE-WALKIES!"

Lenora concentrated all her energies. She pictured the giant going into the gray, disappearing into nothing, she focused everything she had—

"I SAID," the voice boomed, "WHO'S THERE? TELL ME NOW, NOW-DEE-WOW, I'M BEGINNING TO GET ANGRY. MAAAAAAAAD."

"Nothing," Lenora said in a flat voice, as they hurtled ever and ever closer to the giant's huge shoe. "He's not going. I'm having no effect at all."

It had happened again—and at the very worst of times. Her powers had deserted her.

They galloped right up beside the giant's foot, and Coren reached out with his sword. He lunged forward.

"Take that, you fiend!" he cried as he plunged the sword into the shoe. It was as high as he could reach. "For Andilla and honor!"

With a mighty wrench, Coren was swept off the horse. Lenora leaned forward and grabbed for the reins. By the time she managed to get a good grip on them, she found herself some distance down the road. She looked back to see Coren dangling in midair above her. It seemed that the sword had got stuck in the soft leather, and that Coren had obstinately refused to let go of it. The giant had lifted his leg and was trying to shake Coren off.

"Hey, stop that. Hey, hey, hey!" Coren yelled, holding desperately onto the sword as the giant shook his foot around. "Let me down."

With one particularly strong kick Coren flew off the giant's leg, his sword still embedded in the shoe. He landed in a row of cornstalks not far from where Lenora still sat on the horse. Not exactly a soft landing, especially in that heavy suit of armor.

Lenora slipped off the horse and hurried over to him, expecting the worst.

"Never mind," he said between heavy pants, as he gasped for air. "I'm fine. I'm not hurt. I'll stop this giant yet!"

He reminded Lenora a little of her mother's dog, a little white thing, always chasing after dogs three times his size, never fully realizing the danger he was in.

"And exactly what are you going to stop him with, Coren?" Lenora asked.

"Call me Cori. I'll—I'll get my sword back."

"Well, that certainly did you a lot of good the first time," Lenora snorted. "I'm sure that's an excellent plan. And just how do you plan to get it back?" By now, the giant had plucked the offending weapon from his boot and had stuck it in his mouth. He appeared to be using it as a toothpick.

Cori blushed and blustered. "Well then, I'll—I'll—I'll tie him up! Yes, that's it," he declared, his armor creaking as he began to sit up. "I'll get some rope and I'll tie him up, that's what I'll do."

"I don't see any rope," Lenora observed. "And anyway, how do you expect him to stay still long enough for you to tie him up?"

"I have rope, of course," he said, as he leaped to his feet and headed over to the horse. "Knights always have rope. What kind of a hero do you think I am, anyway? I'm *very* good at my job." He gave her a scornful look, then turned and began to rummage around in the saddlebags, carelessly tossing instruments of destruction over his shoulder. Various knives and axes and maces hit the ground with dangerous-sounding clanks and thumps. "And," he added over his shoulder, "I'll *order* him to stand still! He'll just *have* to listen!"

Coren's hands emerged from the saddlebags holding a huge coil of rope. "Aha!" Coren shouted. "I knew this was here! You never know when some rope is going to come in handy when you're out being heroic!"

"Well," Lenora said as she considered the rope, "maybe we can use it. But," she added firmly, "we're going to use our *brains* this time."

"Our brains?" Coren looked bewildered.

All things considered, he really wasn't very much like Coren at all. Maybe she *would* call him that stupid name he wanted.

"Listen, *Cori*," she said patiently, "we'll wait until he gets tired and goes to sleep—he's been awfully busy, and hopefully he'll get tired soon. Then we'll get the rope and tie him up. Just like in a fantasy book I read, about this fellow called Gulliver."

"Yessss," Cori mused. "I guess we could—" Suddenly he paused, in midsentence. "Now hold on a minute, Lenora! *I'm* in charge here. *I'm* going to fell this giant. *I'm—*"

Lenora pinched Cori's cheek so hard he squealed.

"Now you listen to me, young man," she said through clenched teeth, as she glared into his eyes. "You are *not* in charge. We'll do it my way—or you'll be sorry."

For a moment he glared back at her. But she held on and squeezed and glared back, her nose about a millimeter away from his.

Finally his eyes fell. She stopped pinching.

"Well," he said in a quiet voice. "I *am* a gentleman, after all, aren't I? And it's my duty as a gentleman to treat you as if you were a lady—even if you don't act like one. So I will do your bidding, milady." He bowed to her deeply. "But," he added darkly, "I won't like it."

"Good," said Lenora. "Now let's go hide over there in that hay field and see what happens."

"Hide? Me, Prince Coren of Andilla, hide? I do *not* hide!"

She glared at him again. He sighed, then bent over to pick up all his weapons and stuff them back in the saddlebags.

"If he moves," Lenora said, "we'll follow him—quietly, at a distance, so he doesn't know we're there. He'll have to fall asleep sometime."

Sometime turned out to be a long time. It took hours and hours for the giant to fall asleep—he was one frisky giant, no question about it. By the time his eyes actually closed, he'd tromped his way out of the valley where they'd first found him and made his way through two other valleys. Along the way, he'd helped himself to about twenty trees. At one farmhouse, he'd sniffed the air, shrieked gleefully, and then he'd sat himself down and plucked a roof off a barn and ate the entire crop of corn the farmer had stored there. Everywhere he went he left huge pits and crushed buildings from his footfalls. The devastation was terrible.

Lenora and Cori had followed him at a discreet distance, keeping the horse at a slow trot, and bickering constantly. Cori kept remembering various axes and lances he had in the saddlebags that he knew for sure would do the giant in. Lenora kept rejecting his suggestions. They were not a happy pair.

Finally the giant settled down, his head slumped over, and his eyes closed.

"He's asleep," Cori said. He leaped off the horse.

Lenora looked at the heaving mound of flesh draped over the side of the hill and listened to the thunder that seemed to be emerging from it. Snoring. He *was* asleep.

"Now I have a chance to get out my lance and do some damage!" Before Lenora even realized it, Cori had grabbed the sharp-pointed pole from the saddlebags and had begun to run up the hill.

"Come back here this instant, you idiot! You'll ruin everything."

He turned and gave her a withering look—but he came back.

"Take this," she said, and handed him the rope. "We'll start with his feet."

After some difficult climbing, they managed to get the rope around the giant's ankles three times and were making knot after knot to hold the ropes together, when the snoring suddenly stopped, and the giant sat up.

"Uh, oh," Lenora said.

"You are my prisoner!" Cori screamed.

Slowly the giant bent over and saw them at his feet. Then he put out his huge hands and, curling one around Lenora and the other around Cori, lifted them both up in the air.

"WHO-DEE WHOO! WHO ARE YOU?" he asked.

15

Coren didn't like it—it felt like he was running away. He and Lenora—or should he say Leni, as she wanted? Because the more he thought about it, the more it seemed to suit her, these days. Anyway he and Leni were on their horses, slowly trotting away from the castle. King Rayden had tried to convince Coren that going on this trip to the Islands with the princess might help her come to herself, even after Coren had told him about the troubles back home in Andilla.

Oh, Coren knew King Rayden didn't really mean it. It was perfectly clear that for Rayden, Lenora was just one problem too many. No, Rayden wanted her safely out of the way, so he could concentrate on giants and tornados—and on the peculiar plague that appeared to have begun in the East, where the skin and hair of all the citizens of Flang had suddenly become green and refused to turn back again. He wanted Lenora gone, and getting Coren to take her was the best way to get rid of her.

But Coren had agreed to go anyway. Why not? At least it would get Lenora away from that boring Fullbright. Lenora and the councillor did nothing but yammer on endlessly about wedding plans. Lenora hadn't even noticed when the king and

Lufa and twenty or so other powerful minds who knew the north counties had locked themselves in seclusion in the council chamber and then put their minds together to think the giant away. And she had hardly let Coren notice, either. What with the paper flowers and the italics and the pew ribbons, there was hardly a free moment the whole day long.

If Coren had to look at one more paper flower he would scream.

There was one good thing, at least—with the supplies for the cottage filling her mind, Lenora only mentioned the wedding once every two or three minutes now. Although towels and hall runners were just about as exciting as italics and trousseaus.

And, in any case, he had to go. What else could he do? King Rayden seemed to have the giant situation under control, so there was no point in hanging around the castle. He could check in with his parents and find out what was happening in Andilla from anywhere. For a brief moment, he'd considered dropping everything and heading back home. But that would have been foolish. He wasn't going to be able to do anything if his parents and the rest couldn't, as King Rayden had so forcefully told him when Coren had described the situation in Andilla.

"Coren!" It was a voice in his head, calling him as if in answer to his thoughts. It seemed to be coming from a great distance. It sounded like his mother—but so faint he couldn't be sure.

"Mother?" He spoke inside his mind, leaving Leni totally unaware of his conversation—she was far too busy having a conversation with herself about how important it is to know exactly how many sets of silver you own at any given moment, in case of emergency banquets.

"Ah, good, Coren," the voice in his head said, now getting louder. "You heard me! My powers are actually working for once."

It *was* his mother. Thank goodness she was all right.

"All right? Not on your life, Coren, dear. One minute I'm living in a castle, eating good old dragon flambé, and the next I'm sitting at an old wooden table, eating mush."

Coren tried to imagine his mother eating mush. It was almost impossible.

"But I do, I tell you. And I hate mush. Why, there are times I've actually had to resort to speaking! Speaking aloud—can you imagine! It's—it's—unnatural, it's horrible. Sometimes I can't touch minds with *anyone*. I look at them and have no idea what they are thinking." She began to weep. "Oh, Coren, something very strange is going on here."

"My dear, try to get control of yourself." Now his father was there in his mind, too. Coren could see him, taking his mother's hand and patting it.

"You can see how it is, Coren," his father said, his face now turned toward him. "Your mother is a cup of whole wheat flour, two eggs, and a pinch of salt. Drat. Coren, we think you should come home."

"Me? Home?"

"Yes—as soon as possible. All of us here are so disoriented we can't even begin to think about our problem. But you—you're so used to not using your powers that we figure all this—" he waved his arm in an expansive gesture, hardly even noticing that it had turned into a very large stalk of celery— "we figure it wouldn't bother you as much as it does the rest of us."

Well, that was probably true.

"And so perhaps you'll be able to see what's going on more

clearly than we can. Because right now, we're stymied. We awwwwwwwrawk!" His father had turned into a large black crow and was now flying off into the dark corners of Coren's mind, accompanied by his mother, also a crow.

And then they were gone.

And Leni was still chattering.

"Oh, Cori, we'll have so much fun on this trip. It's such an adventure to travel like this, I feel so brave. And it's so wonderful we're going with only two of father's servants, instead of that group of twenty he was going to send. I'm glad he can't spare anyone else now because it's just you and me, practically, and it's so romantic! And, oh, sweetums, I can't wait to see our new home on the Islands. It's all *too* glorious for words."

Coren nodded his head and tried to sort out the confused state of his thoughts.

His parents thought he should go home—and it did make sense, sort of. And it pleased him, too—finally they were having to admit that not using your powers might be a good idea. Sometimes, at least.

But if it was his clear head they wanted, well—why couldn't he just use it from here? That way, at least, he could also keep tabs on the situation with Lenora and what was happening in Gepeth. Because it all had to be connected, somehow.

Unfortunately they'd disappeared now, just blinked out of his head. And he couldn't explain it to them. If he didn't show up back home in Andilla, and soon, they'd be mad at him for not obeying orders. He had to go. He had to tell Leni to go off to the Islands by herself, and then he'd turn around and head off for Andilla.

Maybe, on the other hand, if he just sent his mind out roving, other minds in Gepeth might give him some clues. He might notice something in their thoughts that they wouldn't even think was important, that they wouldn't bother to tell Rayden or the keeper.

Coren sent his mind out, randomly switching from one set of thoughts to another.

What he encountered was mind after mind full of anxiety. Snowstorms, other strange weather—in one county to the west, more than two hundred rainbows had appeared, all at the same time. And just south of the castle there was a little pocket with no weather—no weather at all. The whole idea of weather had just departed from everyone's head.

Elsewhere, strange roads appeared, right in the middle of growing crops, and then just as quickly disappeared again. Some of the roads were peculiarly vast—like two or three roads running right alongside each other, with narrow strips of dirty-looking grass in between.

And people were appearing, too—people and other things. A group of giant snails had suddenly taken over the central square in Padorna, and a gleaming metallic being with many flashing eyes had suddenly shown up in a house in the south counties and started to shout at people, demanding that they insert their cards into its mouth and await further instructions. Nobody knew what cards it meant, but it didn't seem to mind. It kept on shouting the instructions until it blinked out of existence, leaving a small pile of greenish paper behind it.

Elsewhere, gangs of strangely dressed boys terrorized the townsfolk, and bizarre vehicles that looked like insects without wings popped onto the roads and then vanished again. One of them buzzed so loudly as it went by that it deafened a farmer in a nearby field for the rest of the day. His head hurt so much he almost forgot how green his skin and hair were.

And as Coren's mind moved farther north, the giant, always the giant, smashing, sitting on things, stomping on things.

Rayden and his powerful minds obviously hadn't managed to get rid of it. It still filled people's thoughts.

It filled his own thoughts. And before he even realized it was happening, he found himself *in* the mind of the giant. A good idea, that—why hadn't he thought of it before?

Well, Coren had to be honest with himself. It was fear that had prevented him. He had thought of it right from the start. But he could just imagine what sorts of ugly thoughts went on in the mind of a giant. He wasn't sure he could take it. What good would he be to anybody if he became completely terrified?

But he was there now—right in the middle of the giant's thoughts. And it wasn't ugly at all.

Just the opposite, in fact. The giant's head was filled with happy thoughts and songs and with a tremendous joy in all things. It was like the mind of a playful young child—mischievous, perhaps, but certainly not evil.

"HIEDEDLY DIEDEDLY, HIEDEDLY DIEDLEDY DOE! I'D LIKE TO SING A SONG AND DO A SHOW!" it was thinking.

And this was the being who was terrorizing Gepeth?

At this very moment, the giant was puzzled. "WHAT," it was thinking, "ARE THOSE TWO LITTLE INSECTIE-WECTIES TRYING TO DO?" They were tickling his ankles. "TICKKLY WIKKLY WOO." It made him want to laugh.

The giant bent over to get a closer look. And through the giant's eyes Coren saw—himself!

Himself and Lenora!

But it couldn't be. He couldn't be there if he was here—and Lenora was here, too, wasn't she? He turned and looked at the girl beside him.

She beamed at him happily. She was there, all right.

But she was also there in his head, in the giant's view, somewhere far off to the North!

He and Lenora were in two places at once. Somehow, whatever it was that was happening had managed to duplicate both Lenora and him!

He had to find out what was going on. Maybe he could enter the other Coren's mind and find out—something.

He pushed his way into the other Coren's head, expecting only to hear something like an echo of his own thoughts. Another surprise—it was completely different in there.

Well, not completely different. He had all his own memories, it seemed—right up until early on that day when he'd said good-bye to Lenora and left her there in her room. But after that he had other memories.

And other ideas. "Kill," he was thinking. "I want to kill him. I want my lance! I'll rip through his innards and spill them on the ground."

Coren quickly removed himself. Those certainly weren't *his* thoughts.

What about that other Lenora. What was going on in her head?

Coren entered the other Lenora's mind. "It's all that idiot Cori's fault," she was thinking. "No brains. All bravado. I wish the *real* Coren were here." Then she stopped and paused. "Coren? Coren? Is that you?"

He tried to say yes—but no luck. She always knew when he

was in her mind, she could sense it. But he couldn't speak to her like he could to his parents.

"Well," she said, "I *know* you're there. And you have no business in my head, but this time I'll forgive you. I mean, I suppose I did kind of wish for you—just like before, except then it was you but not really you, and look what happened, and, oh, Coren, please, just get here quickly!"

That *was* Lenora. And she was in big trouble.

His parents would have to wait. He'd have to go help her.

And if that was Lenora, then who was this other creature? He turned and stared at Leni. She looked like Lenora. But, he realized, she hadn't been acting anything like Lenora for a long time now. Then who *was* she?

And then it hit him. She was one of Lenora's creations.

Of course—it was the only possible explanation. Lenora had thought her up and left her there while she went off to get rid of the giant.

But why had she left such a *bad* imitation of herself? This awful creature who insisted on calling herself Leni and thought of nothing but tea towels and italics. Surely Lenora could have done a better job of duplicating herself than this?

He glared at Leni disdainfully. Unless—unless Lenora imagined that this was the way Coren wanted her to be.

At that thought, Coren blushed. There was more truth to that than he cared to admit. After all, he hadn't caught on, had he? Not until now.

"Leni," he said, happy at last to call her by her nickname—because she clearly wasn't Lenora, thank goodness, "we aren't going to the Islands."

"What? Oh, don't be silly, Cori, dearest. Of course we are!"

"No, we're not. We have to go rescue Lenora."

"Rescue me? But what do you mean? I don't need to be rescued—except from your manly embrace, Cori, sweetheart." She giggled.

How could he get her to understand?

"Listen, Leni," he said patiently. "You *think* you're Lenora. But you're really not. You're just a creation she made up. You're her, but you aren't her."

"A creation? Made up?" Her eyes narrowed. "Now, hold on a minute there, Prince Coren of Andilla," she said, using his full title with as much disdain as possible. "I *am* Lenora and I know it and you know it and you certainly aren't going to tell me differently."

Coren looked at her impatiently and then made a sudden decision and spurred his horse.

"Oh, yes, I am," he replied, over his shoulder. "You can come with me if you want, or you can go back to the palace."

Leni would be hurt, of course. But it was hard to care all that much about a person who hadn't even existed twenty-four hours earlier.

And who cared more about towels than she did about him.

He called to the servants. "You two return to the palace. Tell King Rayden that the real Lenora is in the north counties and I'm going after her." And with that he galloped off, leaving Leni to fume at his retreating back.

"Well!" Leni exclaimed. She looked at the bewildered servants. "Oh, do as he says," she exploded. "Go and tell them. They'll see he's gone completely mad. I'll go after him to make sure he's all right. He is my fiancé, after all, and I love him completely and absolutely and will follow him anywhere." And she galloped off after him.

16

They traveled all day and all night, stopping only briefly to rest their horses. Coren tried to talk Leni into imagining that the horses were already rested or better yet, that they were in the north counties, but she refused.

"Remember the Balance, Coren, dear," she said, a self-satisfied smirk on her face. And she wouldn't listen when he tried to persuade her that the Balance was already in big, big trouble and that they had to do whatever they could to save it.

"Like go rabbiting off on some thoughtless scheme—with a cottage full of linens to be counted!" she pouted.

She did, however, agree to imagine some light for them to travel by, after her horse stumbled in the growing darkness and nearly tumbled her off onto the gravel—that could have seriously damaged her frock. The light hung in the air some distance above and in front of them, and was almost as good as a full moon.

As they galloped through the eerie semidarkness, Leni kept up a constant whine, telling Coren how cold she was and how sore and how tired, and speaking longingly of all the thick blankets and soft pillows and useful toothbrushes that awaited them at the cottage they weren't going to. Coren reminded her that she could just imagine her teeth brushed and her body warm— an idea that angered her so much that they finally ended up not speaking at all. This gave Coren time to check in with the real Lenora's thoughts.

The giant finally did put her and Cori down, which was a relief. And he put them down gently—Coren had had ugly visions of the giant suddenly losing interest and dropping them. From that height, they would have made a particularly grue-some splat when they landed. But, in fact, the giant was so care-ful that they both touched the ground ever so gently, feet first.

Which was exactly the message Coren had been trying to relay to the giant's mind. He had no idea when it finally hap-pened whether it was his idea or the giant's own.

As the giant grunted and strained to undo the knots and then unwrap the ropes from his ankles, Lenora and the other Coren tried to sneak off. But, apparently, the giant didn't want them to leave. In particular, he didn't want Lenora to leave. Every time she or the other Coren tried to take a few steps away from him, his huge foot or arm shot out and stopped them.

It made Lenora furious. Also the other Coren—Cori, Lenora called him.

"Blast," Cori said. "If only I had my sword back, I'd give him one, right through the toe! My Snetzerland No. 1 battle-ax with the serrated edge and flesh-entering finish would be even better!" But after Cori had tried to sneak over to the horse, the giant had picked up the saddlebags and all their con-tents, swung them around in the air like a sling, and thrown them away. They had landed somewhere over the other side of the hill, out of sight and way beyond Cori's reach.

A good thing, too, Lenora thought. If he kept on sticking

those silly little weapons of his into the giant, the giant might get annoyed enough to give him a big swat, and Cori would be squashed like a flattened spider. Which, in Lenora's opinion, was exactly what he deserved. But it would not have been pretty to look at. All things considered, Cori was better off without the sword.

Meanwhile, Coren was trotting down a road and feeling about as happy as a flattened spider himself, probing the giant's mind, trying to figure out why he wasn't either letting Lenora and her loudmouthed friend go, or else getting rid of them altogether.

But the giant's thoughts were very hard to read. They were an incredible jumble of disconnected images and ideas and rhymes and songs. He certainly didn't have any really bad thoughts. He didn't even seem to be thinking of himself as a powerful giant. At times, in fact, he seemed quite sorry for all the trouble he'd caused—although at other times he seemed to take great pleasure in remembering all the chaos and how much fun it all was.

At one point, Lenora tried to talk to the giant, but his booming voice was so overpoweringly loud and he seemed so confused that she couldn't get anywhere. Every once in a while the giant would pick her up again and bring her up to his face and stare at her, while totally ignoring the bluster and bravado emanating from Cori down below. And then, daintily and ever so carefully, he'd put her down again.

But when the giant stared at Lenora, Coren was startled by the images that were passing through the giant's mind. Surely they couldn't be what they seemed?

Because they seemed like images of elves, of all things! And there were little people in the giant's thoughts, too, and trolls and fairies. And all of them looked exactly like the inhabitants of Grag—the country Coren and Lenora had just returned from a few short weeks ago. There were no giants in Grag, so far as Coren knew. How could this giant know all about Grag?

And yet now, as he stared intently into Lenora's face, the giant's head suddenly filled with a picture of Hevak, the tyrannical ruler of Grag.

There was only one logical explanation. Somehow, in a confused and halting way, this giant was picking up images from Lenora's thoughts—or perhaps even from Coren's thoughts. Perhaps the giant somehow sensed him there, inside his head, and was reading Coren's thoughts as Coren read his.

This was bad news, very bad news. A giant was trouble enough. A giant who could read your thoughts and know what you were planning to do before you even did it was the kind of enemy nobody wanted.

Coren withdrew immediately from the giant's head, before his own presence there became any clearer, and the giant figured out that someone was coming after him.

Someone, indeed. A puny little freckle-faced coward accompanied by a towel-counting girl with colored goo all over her face, both shivering on tired horses and with empty stomachs and unbrushed teeth.

No question about it—your average flattened spider was much happier than Coren.

17

It took only a few more hours of riding to bring Coren and Leni to the cornfield where Lenora was being kept prisoner. As they approached it, the first thing they saw was the giant's head looming over the horizon, some distance down the road.

They reined in their horses and stared at it. It was unbelievably large. And wrinkled. And very scary looking.

And, Coren thought, somehow familiar looking, probably because he'd been seeing it from Lenora's eyes. Or—?

But there was no time to worry about that. He had to do something about getting Lenora away from that monster, and fast.

What, exactly, Coren didn't know. He had no plan at all. And it certainly wasn't easy trying to come up with one as Leni nattered on and on and on about how silly it all was, and how nasty the giant looked, and how they were sure to be squashed like mashed potatoes, and how her hair would be ruined, just *ruined* if that should happen. When Coren did spur his horse and rush off toward the cornfield, it was mostly just to get away from Leni.

And she, of course, followed right on behind him, nattering all the way.

Luckily, the giant was looking in the other direction by the time they got there. He didn't even notice them arrive. In fact, he started to bound away in the other direction.

"Coren!" Lenora yelled as he rode into view. "It's about time you got here!"

"That's quite a welcome," Coren grinned, dismounting from his horse, every muscle sore and aching. "Not even a 'hello' first?"

"Well, I *know* you were reading my mind, and I did ask you to come, didn't I? So, of course, I've been expecting you. And we've been trapped here ever since, you know. I really think you might have hurried."

"I did hurry," he said, indignantly. "I came as fast as I could. Are you all right?"

"I suppose so—as fine as a person can be when they're being kept like a mouse in a trap. He did at least bring us some water, in that huge barrel over there. It's not his fault it had straw in it and other things I'd rather not even mention. But he's not such a *bad* giant, really. Except that he refuses to let us go anywhere—and every time we try he just picks us up and brings us back."

"But he's gone now," Coren said, looking over to where the giant had bent down over a garden and was trying, not very successfully, to pick up tiny little carrots and beets in his clumsy fingers. "We can just leave, right away!"

"No, we can't," Lenora said, gloomily. "We've tried, again and again. As soon as we start he notices us and comes right back and picks us up and plonks us down in this field again."

Coren and Lenora were so busy talking to each other that

they really didn't notice the distress on Cori's and Leni's faces.

"Who are *you*?" Leni finally said, marching up to Lenora and interrupting her conversation with Coren.

"Oh," Lenora said, giving Leni a disdainful look. "It's you, is it?" It was clearly her creation, although it was a little hard to tell with all that clown paint on her face. And that silly hairdo, too. What *was* she thinking of?

One good thing, though—being near her double wasn't bothering Lenora nearly as much as she had imagined it would when she first invented her. Maybe it was because this creature really didn't seem to be like her at all.

Still, her being here was annoying, if it meant what Lenora thought it meant.

Lenora turned back to Coren. "Did you have to bring *her*? You don't really like her *that* much, do you?"

"Like her?" Coren shot back. "Lenora, I can't stand—" suddenly he stopped and looked at Leni. "Uh, I mean . . . Well." He stumbled into silence.

"Hah!" Lenora said. "Just as I thought. You *do* like her. And you claim to want to marry *me*!"

"But Lenora, I—"

"Well," Lenora interrupted. "I don't want her around me, that's for sure. And I can't disappear her, you know, because I seem to have lost my powers. I wish you hadn't brought her."

"Disappear me?" Leni cried. "What do you mean? You can't disappear me! *I'm* the Princess Lenora. Well, I prefer to be called Leni but I *am* Lenora and I *am* the princess and this is Coren, my fiancé, and, well, who are *you*? And why are you wearing that awful outfit? The color is completely wrong for you."

"Awful? Wrong? Listen here, you—you—I'm the *real* Lenora. I *created* you so I could get away and get rid of this giant."

"Created me? You?" huffed Leni. "The very idea." Then she looked up at the giant with trepidation. "And if you wanted to get rid of that," she added, "you haven't done a very good job."

Meanwhile, Cori was staring at Coren. "And who is *this*?"

"I told you already," Lenora said to him, "he's the *real* Coren. I made *you* up, too."

"That puny little thing is supposed to be me, Prince Coren the Bold of Andilla, scourge of all the lands? He doesn't even have a sword. Where's his armor? Get serious."

But Coren didn't even hear him. He was too busy grinning at Lenora. "You missed me!" he said. "You made him up because you missed me!"

"Maybe," Lenora said, a sly smile on her face. "Maybe I did." Then she threw her arms around him. "Yes," she declared, planting a loud kiss on his cheek. "Of course I did, you ninny!"

"I missed you too, Lenora," Coren said, his voice low so the others couldn't hear, "more than you can imagine."

"But," Lenora whispered, "surely you aren't trying to tell me that you didn't like my substitute?" She turned and looked at Leni, who was staring at the embracing couple in shocked astonishment. "Isn't she what you always wanted?"

"I thought so," Coren admitted. "I really did. But she's so boring, Lenora! You've certainly taught me a lesson."

"Well," Lenora grinned, "that's not why I did it, but I'm very happy it had that result." And she kissed him again.

"Come to think of it," Coren said, "how do you like the new me?" He noticed that Cori was glaring at them also, hands on his metal-clad hips.

Lenora looked at Cori and shook her head. "Impossible. I

don't know what I was thinking of. No brains, all brawn."

Coren and Lenora stared at the two others. The others stared back.

"That's *my* fiancée you are touching, *sir*," Cori said between clenched teeth.

"And mine," Leni added. "Get your hands off him, you harlot!"

"Actually," Coren said, delighted to finally be rid of her, "*she's* my fiancée, not you."

"And he's mine, not you, Cori," Lenora added.

Leni and Cori looked at Lenora and Coren and then at each other and then at Lenora and Coren again, utterly bewildered.

"But—but—oh, Coren, darling," Leni whimpered. "How can you do this to me? Desert me for another! And somebody with such bad taste in clothing, too!"

"Why," Cori added, "he doesn't even have a sword! How can you prefer someone who doesn't even have a sword?"

"I'd never desert *you*, Coren," Leni wailed. "Never—not even when there are handsome, adorable fellows like this around!" She gestured toward Cori. "Bold, brave fellows who are twice the man you are! But I haven't even noticed how completely adorable he is, because I'm faithful, and you—you—" she broke down in tears.

"Yes, I *am* adorable, aren't I?" Cori flashed his teeth at Leni. "It's about time that somebody noticed," he added, giving Lenora a dirty look. Then he turned back to Leni. "You are very lovely."

Leni wiped tears from her eyes. "Why, thank you, kind sir. What good manners you have, how knightly—unlike some people I could name."

As Cori and Leni stood simpering at each other, Lenora

raised her eyebrows and shook her head. "What are we going to do with them?" she whispered to Coren.

But Coren had no chance to answer. A loud rumbling noise overhead interrupted their conversation.

"TWINS!" it thundered. "TWINSI-WINSI-WINS!"

The giant had finally noticed them. He was back.

18

The giant's voice was so loud that Coren's hands went up over his ears before he even realized he was doing it.

"He does that all the time," Lenora said, wincing. "He just won't talk in a decent voice. My ears are killing me!"

Coren looked up into the giant's face, his hands still over his ears. As he looked, his eyes widened. Those twinkling eyes! Those wrinkles! And earlier, those memories, Grag— Could it be . . . ?

"And when I try to talk to him," Lenora continued, "he can't seem to hear me properly, no matter how loud I shout."

"Lenora," Coren said in an excited voice, "have you looked at him? I mean, have you *really* looked at him?"

"Well, of course, how could I avoid looking at him, I mean, he's so big, he fills up the—"

"Look now! Look again! His face—isn't it sort of—familiar?"

Lenora stared up into the giant's face.

"Why," she said, her voice filled with surprise. "He looks like—" She turned to Coren in confusion. "But it can't be. It's impossible, he's too—"

"Too big." Coren nodded. "I know. But if he weren't so big?"

"If he weren't so big," Lenora said, "he'd look just like— exactly like—"

"Exactly like one of those little elves we met in Grag!"

"Exactly," Lenora said.

"Exactly," Leni echoed, and so did Cori. Apparently they had the memories of the elves from Grag in their heads, also.

Yes, Lenora thought, staring upward, same leathery skin, same leather breeches, jerkin and boots, and the same pointed ears. He looked like an elf, all right. A *very* big elf.

"It sort of makes sense," Coren mused. "I mean, earlier, I caught some of the thoughts in his head—thoughts of Grag, of Hevak, of our adventures there. I couldn't understand that at all, I thought he was probably reading my thoughts somehow, you know? Exploring my memories? But now that I see him— well, they could just be his own thoughts. It does sort of make sense—or it would if he weren't so huge."

"Coren," Lenora said urgently, "go into his mind again. Maybe there's something there—some explanation."

"Who cares about explanations," Cori yelled. "I've already read his mind while you two were jabbering away and wasting time, and I can see it clearly, he's an elf, all right. An elf from Grag. Just let me at him! No puny little elf is going to pick on me, Coren the Bold, and that's for sure. I'll tame him. I'll—!"

By this time Cori had advanced almost all the way to the pointed tip of the elf's boot. Lenora rushed after him and pulled him back.

"No, you won't," she said, glaring at him angrily. "You've done enough damage already. Now, you just be quiet and let Coren concentrate. Understand?"

Cori glared back at her for a while, and then sullenly backed away.

"Some people," Leni said, "have no appreciation of true heroism." She smiled at Cori.

He smiled back.

Meanwhile, Coren was concentrating on the elf's thoughts. Finally, he opened his eyes and turned to Lenora.

"He's an elf, all right. And he's from Grag."

"I told you that already," Cori said angrily. "Oh, if I only had my medium sword with the titanium edge!"

"Quiet!" Coren snapped, so caught up in his thoughts that he didn't even realize how unlike himself he was acting or notice the belligerent look Cori was giving him.

"That's why he was keeping you here, Lenora," Coren continued. "He recognized you from Grag. You and me—or at least he thought it was me. You and this wild fool with the armor you created are the only thing he's recognized or found familiar since he came here, and he thought that—"

"Wild? Fool?" Cori suddenly interrupted, his eyes shooting fire at Coren. "*You* are calling *me* a fool? Hah! Well, sir, you're just a—a coward!"

"That's telling him," Leni said, giving Cori an admiring gaze. "Just who does he think he is anyway? Not that I won't adore him always and forever, of course, like a good fiancée ought to."

"Will you two stop interrupting?" Lenora said. "This is important. Just shut up and listen to Coren!"

"Shut up?" Leni repeated. "*You're* telling *me* to shut up? Well, let me tell you, I'm not taking orders from somebody who doesn't even know what colors make her skin look sallow!"

Just then, the giant reached down and picked Leni up. He dangled her in midair. She shrieked in terror.

"Put her down, you—you—you giant!" Cori yelled, rushing over and kicking at the soles of the elf's shoes. "Put her down right now!"

But the giant didn't put her down. And Leni continued to scream.

Cori stopped kicking and, grabbing onto a dangling shoelace, climbed right up onto the elf's foot and began to shimmy his way up over the anklebone, punching and shouting as he went. "Put her down!"

Their screams were drowned out by a huge rumbling eruption from the elf's mouth. "HEE! HEE! HEE!" he roared. "OH, TIDDLEE HEE!"

The elf was giggling. Apparently, Cori's vicious punches were tickling his ankle. He didn't want to be tickled. He leaned over, grabbed Cori off his leg, and dangled him in the other hand.

Cori kept right on shouting. Leni screamed. The giant shook them to try to make them stop. They screamed some more.

Amused smiles on their faces, Coren and Lenora looked up at their doubles dangling and shouting overhead.

"Well, at least this way we can talk for a moment," Lenora said. "How did the elf get here? And why is he so big?"

"He doesn't know," Coren said. "It just happened, all of a sudden. One minute he was at home in Grag, dancing around and frolicking, you know, the way the elves always do—and the next minute he was here and huge."

"Just happened," Lenora mused. "Like all the other strange things that have been happening here."

"And in Andilla," Coren said. He quickly told her about what he'd learned from his parents.

"But then," Lenora asked, "why did the elf do all that damage, crush the buildings and everything?"

"He didn't want to, Lenora. He was simply cavorting in his usual way, except now he's so big that he cavorted all over everybody and crushed their buildings. He couldn't control himself. He knows that he's caused a lot of damage and scared people badly, and he feels really sorry about it all. All he wants to do now is go home."

"That's so sad," Lenora said. "We'll have to help him."

"And help ourselves, too," Coren nodded. "And those two up there as well, I suppose," he added, pointing above his head. "One thing's for sure—there isn't going to be any peace here in Gepeth until the elf gets back home to Grag."

Lenora nodded. "The only question is, how will we get him back there?"

Coren shook his head. "I have no idea. No idea at all. Do you?"

Lenora shook her head. "I'm afraid not."

They looked at each other helplessly, listening to the symphony of screams over their heads.

"What I don't understand," Coren finally said, "is why you can't just imagine him back home again. And," he added, "get rid of those two caterwauling ninnies while you're at it."

"I've tried," Lenora said. "Believe me, I've tried. But the giant—the elf, I mean—he seems to be affecting my powers— just like the other strange things did."

"Other strange things?"

She told him about her other unusual encounters, about the cold and about the dragonfly machines and Sayley's horse.

"I wish Lufa were here," she finished. "She's so wise. She'd be able to—" She broke off in midsentence. "Oh, I can hardly think with all this noise. Do you suppose we can get him to put them down?"

"Of course," Coren said, grinning. "He has a compliant mind—if I concentrate hard, I'm sure I can get him to do what I ask. If you're sure you want them down."

"I suppose we have to," Lenora sighed.

Coren nodded and then looked up, putting his hand over his eyes to shield them from the sun.

"Hey, you up there," he shouted. "Cori, is it? If we ask him to let you down, do you promise to behave?"

"No interruptions?" Lenora added, looking directly at the bottom of Leni's feet. "And—" she turned to Cori, who was struggling so much he looked like a puppet on a string—"no silly attempts to fight somebody twenty times your size?"

For a while, Cori and Leni refused to agree. Finally, after Coren entered the elf's mind again and encouraged him to give them some particularly energetic shakings, they both looked very grim and nodded. Then Coren closed his eyes and concentrated as hard as he could, trying to communicate what he wanted to the elf.

After a few moments, the elf frowned. Then, still looking very perplexed, he cupped Leni and Cori into one hand and bent down toward Coren and Lenora and spoke.

"SHOULD I LET THEM GO-DEE-WOE? I WANT TO, I WANT TO!" The words, blasting into their faces at such a close range, nearly knocked them both over. But Lenora regained her footing and nodded, and a moment later the elf had uncupped his hand, and Cori and Leni were down on the ground again, gasping for air and straightening their clothes.

"That's what you get for being so thoughtless," Lenora said.

"Lenora's right," Coren agreed. "He turned to Cori. "Why, if you hadn't been so busy flailing around trying to be a big hero, you might have realized you could have used your powers to get him to put you down all by yourself."

"Well," Leni said, "at least he's brave, Coren, darling, not like—" She stopped in midsentence as she noticed the look Lenora was giving her.

"Remember your promise," Lenora said. Leni said nothing.

For a while there was silence, as Leni and Cori nursed their hurt pride and Lenora and Coren tried, unsuccessfully, to think of a plan.

"We'll just have to take the elf back to the castle," Lenora finally said. "Lufa will help us figure it out. If anybody can, she can."

"That's a *wonderful* idea," Leni snorted. "Taking that huge big lug across the country. He'll stomp on *everything*. Honestly!"

"No, he won't," Cori shouted, also forgetting his promise. "He'll listen to *me*! He'll follow me like a puppy dog if I insist he does! You just watch!" He was already on his feet and waving his fists in the air.

Leni giggled at him. "Oh, Cori," she said, "you're so ferocious!" And she batted her eyelashes at him.

Cori turned to her and blushed. "I'm rather good at my job," he said.

"She has a point," Coren had to admit, "about destroying the countryside, I mean. But the elf seems able to hear my thoughts clearly—much more clearly than you ever do, Lenora. Maybe I could link my mind to his and direct him where to step—if he'd let me ride on his shoulder I could do it for sure. Then he wouldn't step anywhere he shouldn't."

"Now, that's an excellent idea," Lenora said decisively. "And the best thing is, he's so big, he could carry all of us—not just you. And he takes such big steps—we'll be back at the castle in no time."

Cori glared at Lenora. "No way he's picking *me* up again," he said.

"Out of the question," Leni agreed. "Look what he's done to my pleats!" She anxiously patted at her skirt.

"You're right," Coren said, ignoring them and nodding at Lenora. "Why should we take a day to travel when he can walk there in an hour? Let me talk to him."

As Cori and Leni kept on protesting, Coren once more looked up at the elf and concentrated very hard. In no time at all the elf had absorbed Coren's thoughts and began to act on them. His hand suddenly swooped down, and he picked up all four of them, totally ignoring the urgent protestations of Cori and Leni.

After a moment or two of panic, Coren found himself sitting on the elf's right shoulder with Lenora beside him, both of them gripping the thick leather jerkin and holding on for dear life. Coren mentally encouraged the elf to stuff Cori and Leni into the brim of his hat—so that they wouldn't fall out, he said, but it was really to get some distance between the two of them and him and Lenora. It worked, too. The elf's hat was so far from its shoulder that Cori and Leni's endless complaining was but a mere buzz overhead.

And off they went.

19

Coren gazed anxiously ahead and spoke mind to mind to the elf as they walked, telling him where to put his feet down. Sometimes there was no other choice, and a field had to be sacrificed. But Coren tried to keep the elf moving more or less along the roads. The surface did sink a bit under the weight of his tread, but the road didn't suffer too much damage.

As they traveled, the people who saw them ran, screamed, and became rather hysterical. But thanks to Coren's careful guidance, no one got hurt. And even sooner than they'd anticipated, the castle came into view.

Coren told the elf to stop in a large field that was lying fallow, just to the east of the castle. Then the elf, whose name turned out to be Quarto, gently removed them from their perches and placed all of them just by the castle gate. He had to stretch his arms out a little to accomplish that, but Coren didn't want him stomping any closer to the castle than necessary.

By this time, Cori and Leni were so hoarse from shouting and screaming and complaining and generally carrying on like complete idiots, they could hardly even whisper.

"At last," Leni hissed. "Hot running water!" And she raced off toward the gate as fast as she could go, Lenora and Cori at her heels. Lenora wanted to stop Leni from getting there first and claiming to be her. And, by now, Cori seemed to go wherever Leni went. Coren stayed behind by himself to thank Quarto—and also to tell him to wait there and not to move an inch. This time, he spoke aloud, shouting at the top of his voice so that the elf could hear him.

As Lenora, Leni, and Cori rushed toward the castle, the front doors burst open, and a crowd of people poured out. King Rayden and Queen Savet were there, and so were Lufa and Agneth, and, behind them, a large group of courtiers, guardsmen, and servants. They had all heard the monstrous rumbling of the elf's approach and they had hurried out to see what was happening. They stopped short, awestruck, as they caught sight of the giant.

"I told you it wasn't working," Lufa said grimly to Rayden, as she surveyed the giant.

"We weren't concentrating hard enough. If we concentrated a little harder—" Rayden stared at the giant intently, willing it out of existence. Nothing happened.

"It's calamity, disaster, the end of all things," Agneth wailed. "That it should happen in my time as keeper! Oh dear, oh dear, oh dear!"

"I told you I could deal with the giant," Lenora declared triumphantly, as she trotted up to the crowd and smiled into all the worried faces.

"*You* could?" Coren said, as he rushed up, out of breath and panting.

"Well," Lenora conceded, "Coren helped, too.

Actually—" she grinned and gave him a wink—"he's rather good at his job."

As Cori gave Lenora a black look, Coren grinned. "Thank you, milady," he said.

"Oh, yes," said Leni to Coren in a haughty voice. "Be nice to *her*. Treat your own fiancée, who adores you, like dust on a carpet, and meanwhile be ever so sweet to a person who needs to have her colors draped as soon as humanly possible."

King Rayden and Queen Savet stared at them in confusion. They didn't seem to know which to be more upset about—a giant suddenly showing up in their front yard or the fact that there appeared to be two Lenoras and two Corens.

"Some way of dealing with a giant," said Agneth, bitterly. "Inviting it into the front yard! The very idea!"

"Dear," said Queen Savet, turning to Leni, "I don't like to worry you, but, well, you seem to have a duplicate."

"Don't be silly, Mother," Leni said, giving Lenora a disdainful once-over. "She looks nothing like me. Nothing at all."

"Correct," Lenora said. "I don't. Look at that lard on her face. Don't pay any attention to *her*, Mother. *I'm* the real Lenora. She's just a figment of my imagination. A bad figment. I made her up to fool all of you so I could go hunt the giant. And now—" she paused. "Well, it seems I can't get rid of her."

"Can't get rid of her?" Agneth gasped, his face turning white. "But—the Balance—a duplicate— and giants almost in the castle— why, a thing like this could—" He breathed heavily and clutched at his chest.

"Now, Agneth, dear," Lufa said briskly, patting him on the back, "try to control yourself. We can't have the keeper losing his Balance now, can we? What with all the other things that have been happening, a little matter like two of the same person could hardly make much difference."

"It wouldn't, normally," Agneth said darkly between gasps, glaring furiously at Lenora and Leni. "It all depends on exactly who the person is."

"Honestly," Leni said, "don't you people know your own princess when you see her? *She's* the interloper. Oh, I do hope there's lots of hot water."

"Of course!" It was Cori. He had been listening to all of this intently, and now he had suddenly shouted as he grabbed Leni's hands and twirled her around to face him. "You're right, my darling, love of loves! he cried out. "*You* are the true Lenora, not that silly tomboy over there in the dirty jacket!" As the others watched in astonishment, he pulled Leni toward him and gazed into her eyes. "My true betrothed!" he said. "Call me Cori."

"Oh! Cori!" she giggled. "I will. And you call me Leni, oh, my dearest one."

"Oh, my darling!"

"Oh, brother," Lenora mumbled, as Leni and Cori dived into a passionate kiss. Leni was so caught up in the passion of the moment that she didn't even seem to be noticing all the sharp points that stuck out of Cori's armor.

Coren watched them and blushed—it was what he and Lenora might have looked like sometimes, to a stranger passing by.

"And just who is *he*?" King Rayden asked, staring in disbelief at this very unshy person who seemed to be Coren.

"Him?" Lenora said in a distracted voice. "Oh, well, I created *him*, too. By mistake. But never mind *them*, we'll deal with them later. What about the *giant*? Lufa, do you know where he's from?"

Lufa shook her head.

"Well, we do!" Lenora announced, triumphantly. "Coren found out! He's from Grag! And he's really an elf, a tiny little elf!"

"From Grag?" Rayden looked upset.

"Tiny?" Savet said.

"But how did he get here?" Lufa asked.

"He has no idea," Lenora said. "That's why we came back. We thought you might know, Lufa."

The adults all stared at the giant.

"I have no idea," said Lufa. "None at all."

"I suggest we have a conference," King Rayden finally said. "Right now." He glanced over at the giant again. "Will he behave?"

"Oh, yes," said Coren, "I've been communicating with him mentally. He's quite gentle, really. He's just been trying to get home and he doesn't mean to mess things up, but it's hard to see little things like us and our buildings when you're that height. I'll get him to wait and not move any closer. Perhaps, though—" Coren turned to the queen—"someone could take him some food and water?"

"I'll see if any of the servants dare go near him," Queen Savet said, looking over at the giant. "Thank heavens we've begun to order the wedding food. I have a couple of oxen carcasses in the pantry that might do. I was planning to make soup out of them."

"I'd think him up something myself," Lenora said ruefully, "but I seem to have lost my powers ever since I've been around him."

"Well," said Agneth, giving her an angry look, "that's one good thing at least."

Lenora ignored him. "I suppose we should bring these two along," she said, looking at Leni and Cori. They were still entangled in a passionate embrace.

"We'd better," Coren said. "Who knows what mischief they might get into if we leave them on their own? Although, actually, they seem pretty busy at the moment."

Coren and Lenora pulled Cori and Leni apart, paying absolutely no attention at all to their threats and angry protests, and the party proceeded inside.

20

Soon, they were all seated around the large oak table in the main cabinet room. Suddenly a pile of towels appeared in the middle of the table, all neatly folded.

"Towels!" said Leni, "how thoughtful! And so beautifully folded, too."

"Oh, dear," said Queen Savet.

Lenora stared at her mother.

"Mother—did you just imagine all your towels folded?" Lenora asked, incredulous.

"No," her mother said, obviously flustered, "that is, yes. But it shouldn't have happened. I mean, yes, I was thinking that I have all these towels to fold—and as you know, Lenora, normally I do like to fold them myself, because no one else does them quite properly, I don't know why servants can't learn, because it really isn't hard after all, but they can't, and anyway, here I am stuck in this meeting, and I was thinking, wouldn't it be nice if the towels could just get folded properly by themselves and—well—there they are. I didn't actually—"

"So you wished it, and it happened," Lufa interrupted. "Interesting."

"When *I* do it people don't say it's interesting," Lenora objected. "They get very angry!"

"As they should," Agneth said. "Really, your majesty, I'm surprised at you. A woman of your age, and a public official, too!"

"But I didn't mean it," Savet objected, "I—"

"Ooooh!" screamed Leni. As everyone turned to look they could see that she was no longer seated at the table. She was over near the door, lying in a steaming tub of water. Fortunately, she was covered in thick bubbles. But it was clear that she had nothing on underneath them.

"Don't look, don't look, don't anybody look!" she screamed.

Cori leaped to his feet and rushed to stand in front of her, hands outstretched and eyes blazing.

"If anyone looks, I'll kill him," he shouted. Then he spoke to Leni over his shoulder. "What happened, my love of loves?"

"Don't *you* look either, Cori!" she shrieked.

He quickly averted his eyes. "I'm sorry, my turtledove. But how—?"

"I was simply noticing all those wonderful soft towels and dreaming of a nice hot bath," she said. "And now look! I mean, *don't* look, don't, don't, please don't!"

"Everyone seems to have their powers but me," grumbled Lenora.

"Maybe you have them, too, Lenora," Coren said, earnestly. "Maybe it's only the elf who isn't affected by them. And this is all so—so erratic. Everything keeps, well, changing, sort of. Try something."

"All right," Lenora agreed. And she shut her eyes. When she opened them, Leni *and* the bathtub were gone.

"Where is she?" Cori yelled, leaping across the room and grabbing one of the chairs. "I'll make anyone sorry if she's been hurt—very sorry." He thrust the chair legs into the air before him.

"It's back!" Lenora declared excitedly. "It worked! One nuisance down—and one to go!" And she turned toward Cori, who was advancing on her with the chair held high.

"Bring her back," he said in a menacing voice. "Or else." He thrust the chair out at her, its legs nearly meeting her face.

"Go!" she yelled. "Now!"

But nothing happened. Cori kept right on threatening her.

"Why won't you go?" Lenora demanded. "Oh, Coren, why can't I make him go?"

"Actually," Coren said, giving her a sheepish look, "you didn't get rid of Leni, either. I can read her mind—she's still in the castle. Yes, she's in her room, I mean, your room." He turned to Cori. "She's in the tub there, Cori, I promise you. So you can put down that chair and stop threatening Lenora. Right now." He held Cori in his gaze. For a coward, Coren looked awfully determined.

Cori gazed right back at him, still holding the chair up. "Well," he finally said, looking down, "that's what *you* say. But how do I know it's true?"

"Oh, for heaven's sake," Coren said impatiently. "You're supposed to be me, aren't you? Just look in your mind for her."

"Oh," said Cori. "Right. I keep forgetting. Thinking is so boring." He closed his eyes and scrunched up his face.

Suddenly his eyes flew open. "You're right! It's amazing! She's still in the tub, singing away, quite happy now. And she's thinking about me, and about kissing, and she has no clothes on at all and, and—" Suddenly he stopped and blushed bright red. "I—I'm sorry, Leni," he said into the air.

"I know you don't like me reading your mind, I just couldn't—I'll stop, right now." And he put down the chair and sat on it with a loud clank, looking very sheepish.

"What happened to her?" Lenora said. "Did she imagine herself back in my room, or did she somehow go there instead of disappearing like I wanted?"

Nobody said anything. Nobody knew the answer to her question.

Agneth got up from his seat and began to pace. "This is terrible. And it's getting more terrible all the time. The Balance is out of balance and I don't know *where* it will stop."

"Well," Lenora said, "I don't like my powers acting up, but maybe it's a good thing. Maybe it is, because perhaps now you'll all be willing to think of a *new* Balance. The old one wasn't working, you know."

Agneth stopped in midpace. "Not working? The Balance not working? The Balance of Balances, the supreme Edict? This is—it's sacrilege, that's what. It's evil! And from a princess of the realm, too!"

Lenora turned to King Rayden. "But I know it *isn't* working, Father. Oh, Father, you'll never believe what happened to me, what I saw while I was looking for the giant. All the people—the ordinary farmers—they're not happy. Really, they aren't. They don't like the Balance at all, they just pretend to. And not because of the strange events either. I could tell by talking to them that they weren't happy. Who knows—that may even be *why* all the strange things are happening. So we'll have to change things—I mean once we solve this problem and things get back to normal, we'll just have to change what normal is. Won't we, Father? Won't we, Lufa?"

There was silence. King Rayden and Queen Savet and

Lufa all sat looking down at the table, unwilling to meet Lenora's eyes.

"Well, won't we?" Lenora urged. "Won't we have to, now that you know how unhappy everybody is?"

"Well, actually, Lenora," King Rayden finally said in a small voice, still not able to look up at her, "we knew that already. We've always known it."

Lenora was astonished. "What?"

"Imagining people were happy all the time," Agneth said. "Hah! The very idea. This is the ignorance that threatens our very way of life!"

"I—I don't understand, Father," Lenora said.

"You're the keeper, Agneth. You tell her," said King Rayden.

"Indeed, I will," Agneth began. But Lufa interrupted.

"No," said Lufa. "*I'll* tell her. Oh, I told you, Rayden, Savet—*and* you, Agneth. I told you nothing good would come of keeping her in ignorance. And now, this!"

"This?" Lenora looked at Lufa in confusion. "But—the elf and all, the white stuff, the disappearing roads. They're not my fault—are they, Lufa? Surely you don't think—"

"I don't know, dear," Lufa said sadly. "I simply don't. But—well, anything is possible. And you always have had a mind of your own. And if you'd known the truth, well, maybe, just maybe—"

"Known what truth?" Lenora snapped at her.

"Known the way things are." Lufa paused and sighed. "It's like this, Lenora. We know people aren't always happy with the Balance. After all, *you* weren't always happy with it, were you?"

"No, of course not. But everybody always told me I was being silly."

"Well, Lenora, they were lying to you. No one is ever completely happy with the Balance."

"No one? Ever?"

"No one. Not even Keeper Agneth over there, if the whole truth be known."

"But if people aren't completely happy, then why do we keep things this way?" Lenora asked.

"Because we must, of course," Agneth said angrily. "And as for me not liking it, why—"

"Because we must," Lufa interrupted again, in a sad voice. "Because without it things would be, well—like they've come to be lately. Chaotic. Disorganized. Confusing."

"It would be awful," Savet cried. "Simply awful. It *is* simply awful." She shook her head at the table full of folded towels.

"You see, Lenora," Lufa went on, "many Gepethians believe, as you do, that life would be better if they had their own way, if they could only use their powers whenever and however they wanted. Well, we can't have that, can we?"

"Why not?" Lenora said.

"Maybe it *would* be fun, Lenora," Lufa continued. "And maybe it wouldn't. We simply can't take the chance. That's why we have the keeper. That's why we have all the assistant keepers out in the villages, making sure that people don't upset things. That's why we make sure everybody does what they have to."

"But—but what about freedom? What about everybody *agreeing* to keep the Balance, like you always told me?"

"Well, Lenora," Lufa said, "everybody does agree, of course—but sometimes, I'm afraid, it's only because they have to—because, well, because we here in the castle make sure they do."

There was silence. Lenora stared at Lufa and her parents and Agneth in disbelief. "You mean—? You mean to tell me that you people are in charge of everything in the entire country and you push everybody around all the time and always get your own way? Why, you're just a bunch of bullies!"

"Bullies? Bullies!" Agneth sputtered. "The idea, the very—"

"It's for their own good, you know, dear," Rayden said.

"Of course it is," Savet chimed in, nodding.

"It really is, Lenora," Lufa said in a serious voice. "It really and truly is."

"Well," Lenora huffed. "That's easy for you to say, when you're the ones who get to be the bullies. And all those years you got mad at *me* for wanting things my own way! Honestly! I'm so disappointed in you all—especially you, Lufa. I mean, I might have expected *some* people"—she turned and looked disdainfully at her father—"some bullies, to behave like this, but you? And," she added, standing up and glaring at them, "as soon as we get this mess cleaned up, I'm going to change it all! And if any of you try to stop me—"

At that, Rayden, Savet, and Agneth all started trying to reason with her—to explain, cajole, and, failing that, to yell. Lenora yelled back, and soon the room was filled with shouts and threats.

Well, Coren told himself as he surveyed the chaotic scene, this certainly isn't accomplishing anything. Time for a little bit of calming, before things get completely out of hand.

He shut his eyes and began to emanate restful thoughts as quickly and as powerfully as he could. Calm, calm, he thought, be calm. Verrrrry calm.

The shouting stopped, all at once. There, Coren told himself. That ought to do it.

He opened his eyes to total silence—and an empty room. Everybody seemed to have disappeared.

No—not disappeared. He just couldn't see them from where he was sitting. A quick search told him they were still there—slumped down under the table.

"Oh, no!" Coren said aloud. Somehow, his powers had been magnified—he'd calmed them all into unconsciousness!

21

They weren't dead, thank goodness, only asleep. Very deeply asleep. It took all of Coren's mental powers to get Lenora awake enough to respond to him at all.

"Go away, Coren," she finally said drowsily, in between gigantic yawns, "I'm having the (yawn) most wonderful dream (yawn) about towels dancing (yawn) in a bathtub, and a great hero who's rather—um—good at (yawn)—" And her lids fell over her eyes and she fell asleep again.

Obviously, Coren told himself, mental powers aren't going to be enough.

On the other hand, the bucket of water he went out into the courtyard to get and then threw over her head worked very well indeed. So well, in fact, that she was awake enough to land three very good punches before he got her to stop and he could explain why he had to do it.

Not to mention the water she managed to splash all over him from her soaked hair. Fortunately, there were lots of towels, close at hand.

"You're right, Coren," she said as she vigorously toweled her hair. "I mean, assuming you're telling the truth—" she turned to him, her eyes narrowing— "which you'd better be."

"I am," he assured her. "Honestly, I only wanted to help everyone calm down."

"Well, it's clear that our powers are working erratically— sometimes we can control them, and sometimes we can't."

"And sometimes, it seems, we don't have them at all—just like when we were in Grag, and Hevak—"

"But it's not like that, is it? Because we do have them sometimes. Actually, it seems to be just the opposite of what happened in Grag. There, somebody was controlling us. But here nobody seems to be controlling anything. It's just—random, sort of. Like all the order and control in the whole world is disappearing, somehow."

"Yes, that seems right. Like—" he gave her a strange look— "like there is no Balance anymore."

She glared at him, and then sighed and nodded. "Yes," she said. "That's it. No Balance at all. But what could be causing it?"

They continued to think about it as they shook the others, splashed water on them, and finally got them awake again.

All except Cori. Somehow he seemed much safer sleeping.

As soon as Lufa was awake enough, Lenora told her about their new theory.

Lufa nodded. "That's just what I was thinking. Oh, if only—"

The room suddenly became crowded with people— women. Women of all shapes, sizes, ages, dressed in robes, or elaborate costumes, headdresses made from flowers and real fruit, some with almost no clothes on at all, and everyone talking at once.

"Oh!" said Lufa, shouting above the din. "I think this is my fault. I was wishing I could consult with the other wise women I know—" She stared at the crowd in dismay.

One voice suddenly emerged over the hubbub—it was a rich soprano, singing so piercingly and so loudly that it cut right through the din.

"♪ Lufa ♪, darling," the soprano voice trilled, "so ♪♪♪ glad you ♪ called calledcalledcalled callllled ♪. It's a madhouse in ♪ Pompour. Strange things happening ♪ happening—people actually talking instead of singing or playing to each o—o—o—ther, all our music evaporating. Oh ♪ Lu—u—u—fa, you brought us ♪ here ♪ here ♪ here, did you, my ♪ dear, ♪ dear, ♪ dear? Good ♪ thinking. Perhaps if we all put our minds together ♪, we could—"

Abruptly the voice cut off, and the singer disappeared—along with all the rest of the women.

"I was just wishing," King Rayden admitted, "that they were somewhere else. I do hate sopranos, don't you?"

"Not at all," said Lufa, giving him an exasperated look. "A well-trained soprano is a treat, as any true connoisseur knows. Where exactly did you wish them?"

"Actually"—he looked rather sheepish—"at the bottom of the sea!"

"Really, Rayden," said Lufa. "The very idea!" She snapped her fingers.

Suddenly the women all reappeared, but this time sopping wet.

"I'm so sorry," said the king as he handed out towels. Queen Savet's accident was turning out to have been a good idea.

"Find them quarters and dry clothes," Rayden said to a servant.

"We'll have to have a banquet tonight," fretted Queen Savet. "So many people to entertain!"

"Never mind, Mother," said Lenora, "I'll dream up a wonderful banquet dinner. You won't have to lift a finger."

"Nonsense," said Queen Savet. "We'll do it like we always do. Please excuse me, I have a dinner to see to. What I will do for soup I don't know, now that those oxen are gone. I suppose it'll have to be chicken."

And then the room was overrun with chickens squawking and running and servants chasing them with very sharp knives.

"HELLO-EE OO-EE," boomed a loud voice through the window. Quarto's giant eye appeared on the other side of the glass.

"This meeting," screamed the king, "is temporarily adjourned."

"Dinner at eight," yelled Queen Savet as she backed away from the window in horror and nearly tripped over a chicken. "Dress will be—optional," she said, eyeing all the women nervously.

Servants poured into the room. Some gathered up wet towels. Others ran after the chickens. Cori snored. Lenora went over to the window and shouted at Quarto to get back to his field, right now, before he broke something.

And in the middle of it all, a voice suddenly screamed.

"CORRRENNN!" It was King Arno, shouting as loud as he possibly could.

As Coren winced, he could see that nobody else in the room had even noticed. His father was calling him mentally, inside his mind.

Why, then, was he shouting so loud?

Probably, Coren told himself with a pang of guilt, because he was absolutely furious with Coren. He'd been asked to go back to Andilla and help out there—and that was yesterday, wasn't it? Yes, a whole day ago. And he hadn't even put a foot out of Gepeth yet.

In fact, so much had been happening in Gepeth that he'd hardly even given a thought to Andilla—had almost forgotten about it. And all this time, his family and his country were in danger. The least he could have done was try to keep in mental contact. Coren felt terrible.

"Father," he called out mentally. "I'm sorry. I hadn't realized it was so long. Things have been so busy here—"

"So long? What are you talking about, Coren? I just lost contact is all. It's only been a couple of seconds. Now, as I was saying, things are getting pretty bad, and I want you to come home right away."

A couple of seconds? Only a couple of seconds had passed in Andilla, while a whole day had gone by in Gepeth? It was impossible.

Well, Coren told himself with a sinking feeling, these days, nothing was impossible. As if it wasn't bad enough that giants were showing up and he could put people into deep sleep with a single calming thought—now time was going out of sync, too.

Still, on the bright side, he didn't have to feel bad about forgetting Andilla. It couldn't have been in Coren's thoughts, because it didn't exist in time.

His father's thoughts seemed to come in bursts as his powers worked or failed. Was it something about a dragon breathing flame? A real dragon, in Andilla? Surely not.

"A dragon!" It was Cori, who suddenly awoke with a start, tossed a chicken off his head, and leaped to his feet. "An opponent worthy of me, finally! I'll make flambé out of him, you wait and see! I'll do it, Father, I'll be there as soon as I can! Coren the Bold to the rescue! Now where does King Rayden keep his weapons? A double-edged Berkheimer Masticator, I think, and a grade 2E battle-ax with a tempered hardwood handle." And he ran from the room in a rush.

"No, no," shouted Coren, "wait a minute, you can't—"

But it was too late. Cori was gone.

"Coren, my lad," Rayden said in Coren's mind, "it's happening again. The powers are out of control. Now I seem to be hearing an echo of your thoughts—almost as if you were thinking two entirely different things at once. But I'm glad to hear you'll come. We'll expect you soon. And now I must go." And he blinked out.

Oh, wonderful, Coren thought. Now that madman is off to slay a dragon! He'll probably create even more chaos in Andilla than there is already. And I didn't even get a chance to tell father about him. Should I go after him? Should I stay here and help the rest? I need to talk to Lenora.

But as he turned toward Lenora, Leni rushed into the room, wearing an elaborate gown with layers of skirts and huge puffed sleeves.

"Cori, my darling Cori!" she announced. "I am bathed and dressed and ready to dine." Then she stopped and looked around the room. "Where is he? Where *is* the darling boy?"

"Darling boy?" said Lenora. "Oh, Cori, you mean? He rushed out a minute ago. Said something about slaying a dragon, I think."

"Yes," Coren added, "in Andilla." He turned urgently to Lenora. "My father just communicated and said there are reports of a dragon in Andilla. He wanted me to go and—"

"A dragon! Andilla! Oh, that brave, silly boy!" Leni exclaimed. "I must stop him!" And she turned and rushed out, calling, "A horse! A horse! I need a horse!"

"Yes, do that!" Coren called after her as she hurried away. Not that there was much hope that she could stop Cori, but there was no harm in her trying.

"Oh, Lenora," he said, "I don't know what to do. Should I go after him? Should *I* go to Andilla?"

Lenora thought about it for a minute. "Let him go, I say—it'll take him a few days to get there, and meanwhile he'll be safe and out of our hair."

Coren nodded. "*And* her. But if Andilla is really in danger—"

"If Andilla is really in danger," she interrupted, "it's only because the whole world is in danger. The same kinds of things are happening there as are happening here. Aren't they?"

"Well, yes, but—"

"But nothing. And if we're going to stop it, it won't be by running off half crazed without knowing why or what we're going to do when we get there, like that idiot Cori."

"You mean," he grinned, "you believe we should think before we act?"

Lenora ignored Coren's teasing and grabbed his hand. "Let's get out of here. We need a quiet place to think."

No sooner had she spoken than they were on top of a very high mountain overlooking an unknown landscape, with no one in sight.

"Well," said Coren, "this is certainly quiet."

"Blast," said Lenora, "it's not what I meant at all. Let me try again."

Instantly they were in their own private arbor, the one Lenora had created as their special place. Coren wasn't sure if it existed anywhere in the castle or if they were outside of time and space when they were there, but for the moment he didn't care. It was quiet, peaceful, beautiful. A cool drink appeared in his hand. He drank. Grapefruit juice with shaved ice. Perfect. He smiled at Lenora. She smiled back. Inexplicably, her powers had worked! Still, she didn't want to think about why yet—she had something more pressing on her mind.

"I'm starved," Lenora said.

"Me, too," Coren agreed.

"The banquet is hours away," she said.

"Hours," he repeated.

In front of them appeared a table laid out with fruit, salads, thick hot breads, creamy butter, cheese, and lots of sweets and cakes. Her powers were working very well indeed!

"Let's eat first and think later!" Lenora mumbled, her mouth already full of cake.

And despite all his worrying about Andilla and about Cori, Coren couldn't resist. He hadn't eaten for what seemed like months. His head would work better on a full stomach. He dug in.

22

Lenora woke up with a start. Oh, no! She'd dozed off and so had Coren—who was still asleep peacefully beside her. She gazed at him for a moment. He really was quite handsome. Much more handsome than that fool Cori. Amazing how the same face could look so different with a different personality behind it. She had to admit she was very fond of Coren, crazy about him, really—just the way he was. She bent to wake him with a kiss—and that's when he disappeared. Completely.

"Not again!" Lenora exclaimed, thinking back to a few weeks ago when Hevak had disappeared him just like that, one minute here, the next, gone.

But Hevak wasn't here and now, neither was Coren. She called his name, but that seemed useless, so she imagined the arbor away and put herself in the conference room. Maybe Lufa could help, or her father.

The conference room was empty, too.

Well, perhaps they were all at the grand dinner her mother had been planning. She hurried down the corridor. Maybe one of them had unconsciously wished Coren there and because of the way their powers were working, in a very uncontrolled fashion, Coren had appeared at the banquet on command.

It certainly was quiet in the corridors. Lenora ran down the central staircase to the main floor and then headed for the ballroom. She flung the doors open—nothing! No one! There was food, some of it still steaming in the serving dishes. But not a soul there to eat it.

"Curiouser and curiouser," she muttered, repeating a line from one of her favorite old stories. "Curiouser and curiouser."

"Ho!" she yelled. "Where is everybody?"

Silence.

Perhaps, she thought suddenly, they were all outside with the giant. She raced down the hallway, pushed open the great wood doors, and looked around. It was getting dark, but she could see that there was no giant sitting far away in the field. He was gone, too.

If the giant was gone, the inhabitants of the castle probably weren't in the field either. Still, she had to check. So she ran over to the field—and found it, too, empty.

Lenora stood in the empty field, the sun setting on the horizon, hands on her hips, totally perplexed. *Where* could they all have gone? Then another thought struck her. Maybe they hadn't gone anywhere. Maybe *she* had. Maybe she'd unconsciously imagined herself into an empty world. Maybe everyone was eating and drinking in the castle but *she* was somewhere else.

Well, whatever the reason, she was completely alone. And she didn't like it.

Still, she reasoned, as slowly she made her way back to the castle, if she had imagined herself somewhere else, all she had to do was imagine herself back. She did. Nothing happened.

She walked through the streets of the village. It was empty, as was the castle. She wandered into the banquet hall and stood there, at a complete loss about what to do.

It was so horribly quiet. Lenora felt panic growing inside her—a kind of panic she had never felt before. Perhaps they were *all* alone in their own worlds—each in a totally separate place. What if she were left here, all alone, forever! That would be the worst thing she could ever imagine. No one to fight with, no one to order about. She thought about Coren. No one to kiss. No one to love.

Lenora suddenly realized that she was crying. Just like a little child.

"This is ridiculous," she exclaimed aloud, as she wiped the tears from her cheeks—and hearing her own voice made her feel better. "I'm *not* helpless, I'm not. Let's see—maybe there are people in the countryside. After all, it could be only the people here who have temporarily disappeared."

She didn't hesitate. She marched down the empty corridors and out on the road. But where should she go? Which direction should she take?

Somehow it seemed obvious—she didn't know why, but it seemed as if there were really only one way to go. Without even realizing she was doing it, she'd begun to retrace the route she'd set out on only a few days earlier.

She'd had so much hope then and so much confidence. I was going to get rid of the giant and save the whole country all by myself, she thought ruefully. And now look at me. I *am* all by myself.

Luckily, there was a full moon and the stars shone in the clear sky so she could see quite easily—not that there was ever anyone to see. She hoped as she walked that she wouldn't encounter heavy winds like the ones Lufa and Coren had told her about, or that awful cold white substance—and she didn't.

Nothing changed at all. Just the endless, empty road and the bright stars. Her feet kept plodding onward, as if pulled by some invisible magnet. Well, it was better than standing around and feeling sorry for yourself and doing nothing.

As dawn broke, Lenora began to recognize her surroundings. That tree—yes, it was the one she'd napped under that very first day. And, yes, over there—that was the farmhouse where she'd escaped from the awful cold.

It looked so cozy, that cottage—so inviting. That family had helped her—until they'd started getting scared of her and sent her away. And Sayley had obviously liked her a lot.

Well, she couldn't walk past it without checking to see if anyone was there. She *had* to go in and look.

She headed across the fields toward the farmhouse, moving faster and faster the closer she got. She needed to be in that house, she desperately needed to be there, and as soon as possible. She ran the final few yards to the house, took the steps two at a time, and began to pound on the door.

"Is anyone there?" she yelled. "Open up! Anyone home? Open up! Hello! Hello!" And then, although no one answered, she couldn't help herself. She grabbed at the doorknob, pulled the door open, and peeked inside.

"Leteshia? Is that you?" A little face peered from a door on the other side of the room, and then a small figure ran toward Lenora and leaped into her arms. "Oh, I knew you'd come, I just knew it! And here you are!"

It was Sayley. And here she was, yet everyone *else* seemed to have disappeared. Could she have anything to do with all this?

Lenora put Sayley back down on the floor and looked into her eyes. "Sayley," she asked, "you don't happen to know where everyone is, by any chance?"

At that Sayley stiffened and looked very frightened and then began to cry.

"Sayley? Can you answer me?" Lenora knelt beside the child, whose cries quickly turned into deep, anguished sobs.

"Sayley? Come on. You can tell me. Maybe I can help find them if you tell me."

Sayley's sobs stopped in midgasp.

"Could you?" she asked, lifting her tear-stained face to Lenora's. "Could you find them, do you think?"

"Well, I can't *promise*," Lenora said, "but if you know where your family is that's certainly more than I know."

"But I *don't* know," Sayley wailed. "That's just it. And it's all my fault."

"Your fault?" said Lenora. "How can it be your fault? Now, Sayley, you must calm down like a big girl and talk to me sensibly. We're both very clever and I'm sure if we approach this calmly, and if we think clearly, we'll be able to solve this problem."

Lenora wasn't sure who she was trying to convince—herself or Sayley. Inside she felt like throwing herself on the ground and crying *her* eyes out.

But there was no time for that. Lenora took a crocheted cloth from one of the chairs and wiped Sayley's face. Then she sat the little girl down on the sofa and she sat beside her.

"Now," said Lenora, "since you and I seem to be the only people around, I think it's very important for us to talk. First— *are* you the only person here?"

Sayley nodded. "Yes."

Lenora's heart sank. "Do you know where everyone else is?"

Sayley shook her head. "No."

"Do you have any *idea* where they are?"

Again, "No."

"Then, Sayley," Lenora asked gently, "what did you mean when you said it was all your fault?"

Sayley bit her lip. "I—I—I made them go away. I just thought it—and, and—it happened."

Lenora looked at the child skeptically. Surely this little thing couldn't have such powers. Only Lenora herself could do such things.

On the other hand, if she'd been practicing—and then, with everything out of balance this way—well, maybe, somehow, she *did* do something.

"All right, Sayley," said Lenora. "Tell me *exactly* what happened."

"Well," said Sayley, "after those nasty men did that awful thing to my horse, I imagined myself right back here. I wanted my mother and my father. I wanted a hug. And when they saw me—well, all they did was yell at me and go on and on about the Balance. 'Praise the Balance, praise the Balance,' that's all they could say to me, again and again and again. And then they sent me to bed without any supper. They're such bullies, Leteshia! It made me mad!"

"I'm sure it did." Lenora had to hide a smile. This certainly sounded familiar.

"But I showed them! I made myself a big dish of ice cream, right in my bedroom, and I kept filling it with different flavors, and I ate them all! And I didn't go to sleep at all. I made myself a little circus all in miniature and I watched them do their acts. That was fun! Except when the cat caught the lion tamer and I had to disappear him before he got swallowed. And then I created an entire roomful of wonderful clothes to wear, all in colors that didn't match! That was *lots* of fun. But that was when Mother came to check on me and started yelling at me again.

And they said I couldn't ever use my powers again. And I told them I would! And they said they'd send me away to some awful school if I didn't behave and I said *you*, Leteshia, were the only one who could ever understand me and I wished that there was only you and me left in the whole world because *you'd* be nice to me and I wanted to be with you, nobody but you, and then they all disappeared."

She paused. "And here you are, so my wish must've come true."

Yes, thought Lenora, it must have. No wonder she'd felt drawn here—Sayley had one powerful imagination, no doubt about it. Surely *she* couldn't be responsible for everything else that was happening? A little thing like her? Surely not.

"And," Sayley wailed, "I've killed everyone and they were right and I *never* should have used my powers." At this Sayley's face began to crumple and she began to cry once more.

Lenora let out a huge sigh and leaned back against the sofa.

"It's all right, Sayley," Lenora said. "If you made everyone disappear, you can make them appear again."

"But I can't!" she screamed. "I've tried. I can't!"

Apparently her powers were erratic, too. So it wasn't her fault? But maybe—

"Maybe, Sayley, maybe you just need some help. Together we can do it. I know we can." Lenora took Sayley's hands. "Now, you've probably been too upset to focus properly, that's all. But I'm here and I'm telling you all you have to do is concentrate. And I'll concentrate with you. And everyone will be back, just like before." And madder than ever, Lenora thought to herself, but I'd better not mention that now.

If, she also added, it works at all.

Grasping Sayley's hands in hers, Lenora looked into the

child's eyes. "Now think, Sayley, think very hard. See your family in your head, as clear as can be, and I'll imagine the castle in my head, and we'll just hope that the rest of Gepeth will appear along with them. Think now, think!"

And Lenora thought and so did Sayley. "Fine," said Lenora, "we're going to bring them back. Imagine them all here! Now!"

And suddenly the room was filled with Sayley's family, all talking at once, and Sayley threw her arms around Lenora and gave her a big hug.

23

Sayley's parents immediately began to scold her.

"It was you, wasn't it?" her mother said, hands on hips. "Sayley, how many times—"

Just like home, thought Lenora. And then, she very much wanted to *be* home—to see if her family and Coren had come back also. But Sayley had grabbed her hand and obviously had no intention of letting go.

"I wish," Sayley whispered, "I were somewhere else. This lecture will go on all day."

Suddenly the two of them were in the castle—in the main entrance just inside the big front door.

Lenora grinned at Sayley. When the two of them wished something together, it obviously created a lot of power. Why, anything might happen—anything at all.

Anything at all *had* been happening. Could it be that—?

But first things first. Lenora's main question was answered—she was already hearing the usual noise and activity of the palace. Servants were running past her this way and that, carrying food and utensils, and she could hear voices from the conference room nearby. But it was Coren she really wanted to check on. Was he still in their arbor? Holding onto Sayley's hand, she imagined the two of them there—and found Coren staring morosely at the remains of the food on the table.

"Coren!"

"Lenora! I've been so worried!" He leaped up and gave her a hug that surprised her with its intensity.

"Lenora?" Sayley said. "Her name is Leteshia, not Lenora."

Coren didn't even hear her. "I've been stuck here all alone," he said, "and I couldn't find anyone's thoughts—it's been awful!"

"I didn't mean to do it, not really," Sayley said.

"What?" Now Coren turned to look at Lenora's companion. "Who's she?"

"I'll explain later," Lenora assured him. "I'm just glad you're here. Now let's go check on my parents." With that she thought them all into the banquet room, which was full of people, including the king and the queen.

"It was you, Lenora, wasn't it?" her mother accused her.

"Her name is Leteshia," Sayley said.

"Lenora," Queen Savet continued, "how many times—"

Sayley giggled. "This is just like at home," she said. And then she caught sight of the food. "Except for that."

"Go on," said Lenora, "help yourself."

Sayley was delighted to do just that, leaving Lenora to explain what had happened, which she did as quickly as possible.

"And that's that." Lenora helped herself to a chicken wing as she finished talking. "That's how Sayley and I brought you all back. She *is* a clever little girl." Lenora turned to where Sayley sat behind a plate piled high with food, munching away, and gave her an approving glance.

"But," Lenora added, turning back to her parents, "where were you all this time? Where did you go?"

"Not that awful gray place you usually send me to when *you* imagine an empty castle," her mother responded.

"No," her father agreed, "it certainly wasn't there."

"Well, where was it?" Lenora asked.

Everyone looked confused. "It's hard to say," her father finally replied.

Lufa spoke. "We seemed to be in a strange world where we communicated mind to mind—as Coren always does, I suppose. There were more minds than I imagined possible. And we still had our other powers as well."

"And I must say," Savet said, "some of you do think the vilest things imaginable. You ought to be ashamed of yourselves. I hated it. Chaos. That's what it was. Pure chaos. The worst part was the singing all the time."

"And whaaat ♪," sang one of the wise women, "is that ♪ supposed to mean?"

"I wonder," Lenora mused, "why you ended up there and not in the gray."

"Well," Coren suggested, "maybe there's some connection between that place and all the things that have been happening here."

"It could have been an accident, of course," Lufa said. "Considering all the randomness."

"Yes," Rayden agreed, "I mean, this child, Sayley—nice name, Sayley—she didn't really know what she was doing when she imagined us all away."

"But," one of the wise women interjected, "would a mere child have the power to imagine us all away if everything weren't out of balance already?"

Agneth spoke, looking even more annoyed than he usually did. "You're probably right, Grundilla. And I don't like it. That awful place we went to is much too familiar to me."

"Familiar?" Rayden asked. "What do you mean, Agneth?"

"It's in the Recordings, of course—the old books describing the world as it used to be, before."

"Before?" Lenora said. "Before what?"

"Why, before the Balance. The Dark Evil time. Before our ancestors agreed to the Balance."

Nobody said anything. And then they all began to speak at once.

Coren found it almost impossible to think in the middle of the hubbub.

"Read my thoughts," an urgent voice whispered in his ear. It was Lenora. He leaned over to where she stood beside him. She *actually* wanted him to read her thoughts? The world *was* falling apart.

He read her thoughts.

"Ah, good, you're there, Coren, I can feel it. Listen—I have an idea, but I'm not going to tell *them* about it, because they'll just say no, like always. Are you hearing this?"

He looked into her face and nodded.

"Good," she said inside his mind. "What I'm thinking is, there must be clues to this mystery there—back in the past, before the Balance. So why don't we go there? You and me, I mean."

Coren considered it. It wasn't a bad plan, really. If the world had once been like this before, and the people back then found out some way to do something about it, well, then, maybe—but how could they get back there?

"Oh," Lenora's voice echoed through his mind, "I know what you're thinking, Coren!" And suddenly she could. She could hear his thoughts quite plainly. "You're wondering how we're going to get there."

He looked at her, shocked.

"That's simple. I'll just imagine us there, back in the past. It'll be fun to go back into history. I wonder why I've never thought of it before."

"And what makes you think I'd let you go there?" King Rayden suddenly demanded.

Lenora turned to her father.

"Father—you—you could hear my thoughts?"

For a moment, Rayden looked confused. "Why, yes," he finally said. "I suppose I could. I still can. And I am not an interfering old fool, Lenora."

"Well," she said, blushing, "I suppose it's not your fault. But there, you see—it keeps on happening. The Balance is falling apart. If we don't try to do something—well, anything could happen."

"She's right, Rayden," Lufa said, as a light rain began to fall from the ceiling. "Maybe there is some clue back in the past."

"Yes," a number of the wise women nodded as they put napkins on their heads to keep them dry. "True."

"Perhaps," Rayden said.

"But," Savet interjected, as she looked at her increasingly damp room in dismay, "surely no one actually has to go back there, do they? It's so dangerous. It's so frightening. Couldn't Agneth just look it up in his old records?"

"Of course I can, milady," said Agneth, shaking water out of his hair. "But you must be patient—it will take some time. I have to undergo the Baths of Purification first. And then, once cleansed of all worldly thought and imbalance, I must say the Rituals of Opening, and then there's the Beatification of the

Balance before I can break the seals. And as I turn the pages, I must enact the—"

"Go, Agneth," Rayden interrupted. "Now. Go do what you have to do. The sooner you begin, the better."

"Yes, milord," Agneth said. "I shall begin the ceremonies. Let the Baths be poured. I shall return with the secret knowledge of the Great Histories—for the good of the universe. And as you await me, all should meditate, all should cleanse their minds in preparation for the Mysteries." He swept out of the room, splashing up water from the puddles. At which point, for no obvious reason, the rain stopped, as quickly as it had begun.

"He certainly can be tiresome," Rayden muttered. Lenora was astonished to hear her father say what she was thinking herself—until she realized she had heard the words only in her mind.

"Why, Father," she thought back, hoping he could still hear her. "I'm surprised at you."

"What? Oh, Lenora, it's you in my mind again. Don't do that!"

"You know, Father, I'd wager that you can't stand this sitting around and waiting any more than I can."

"Don't be silly, Lenora," he thought—but underneath it, she caught another thought—the directly opposite one. He was dying to make something happen, fast.

"So," she said, "why not let me go anyway? I could be back in no time—hours before Agneth has even begun his silly ceremonies. We really can't sit here and do nothing."

In astonishment, Lenora realized that Rayden was agreeing with everything she said. In fact, he was thinking how much fun it might be to go along with her himself.

She didn't like that idea at all—going off on an exciting adventure into unknown territory with your father. He'd probably do all the interesting stuff and spoil all the fun.

"No," she thought urgently. "I mean, of course, I'd love to have you with me, Father, but with all your power, wouldn't it be wiser if you stayed behind here, ready to bring me back? In case something goes wrong, I mean—we wouldn't want both of us stuck there in the past."

She could feel his spirits sink. "I suppose so," he thought.

"Good, I'll just take Coren along instead."

"Excuse me," Coren piped up, sending the thought into both their heads. "Isn't anyone going to bother to ask me? Why should I have to go, too?"

"Just because," Lenora snapped. "I want you there."

"Yes," Rayden agreed. "Of course, my lad, you'll go with her and make sure she doesn't do anything incredibly foolish. I count on you to have some sense, Coren."

"Me, too," Lufa suddenly said, aloud. Apparently she'd been listening to the entire conversation in her head also.

And as Coren looked, all the rest of the wise women nodded.

"You're right, Lufa," they agreed.

All this traffic in his head—it was worse than a public meeting back home in Andilla.

Which was still very much on his mind. How were his parents coping? Had there really been a dragon?

But Lenora had been right all along. The best way to try to deal with the problem was to stay here with her. Or go back into the past with her, if that was what she wanted.

Coren nodded, resigned. Lenora had managed to do it again. Put both of them in a dangerous situation. Except somehow she'd even managed to get her father and the normally sensible Lufa to agree with her. This was really too much.

24

I'll call you back in an hour," Rayden shouted. "Don't let her do anything foolish, Coren."

They were holding hands and hurtling through a void, a space so empty it didn't even have a color or a shape, as Rayden's words gradually disappeared into the distance.

Then, out of the void, a shape appeared and moved toward them.

"I DIDN'T MOVE, COREN-WOREN," the shape screamed. "I KEPT MY PROMISE, I DID, I DID, I DIDDLY DID. IT WAS THE WORLD THAT MOVED AWAY FROM ME. FIDDLY FEE."

It was Quarto, the giant elf, tumbling through the void beside them. In this empty space, it was hard to tell exactly how large he was. Why was he there? Had they started off another outburst of unbalance?

And what would the people in the past do when they saw a giant in their midst?

All at once, the void filled, and a world was there, all around them.

A very familiar world. A large square surrounded by

magnificent buildings covered in ornate statues and balustrades and golden decorations that glinted in the sun.

It was Grag. It was the central square of the city of Farren in the country of Grag. Grag, where they had had their adventure only a few short weeks ago. Where Quarto the elf came from.

And Quarto was there with them, a giant no more. He had somehow returned to his regular size and was now perched on Lenora's shoulder.

"Oh, what a relief!" he trilled in his tinkly, elfish voice, looking out over the square of his home city. "Bliss-a-damissima! You know, I much prefer being the little one in a land of biggety-big people than the other way around. Boundie-rounda-la-bound!" And he did a handstand on Lenora's shoulder and then leaped to the ground.

"Well, this is just wonderful!" Lenora exclaimed. "We try to go to the past and end up in Grag instead. Honestly, if we can't control anything, how are we going to fix anything!"

She looked around and immediately noticed that, although this was certainly Grag, it was a very different place than the one she had known. The courtyard, for instance, had quite a different character. Before, everything had been clean, white, pristine. Now streamers and colored cloth festooned the huge white pillars of the palace. The courtyard floor was a sparkling array of blue and silver tile, and filling it were booths where little people, big people, elves, trolls, and fairies bartered, talked, laughed, shouted, and even sang and danced. Was it the past after all? Or—?

"What's happened here?" Lenora said to Coren, finding the change hard to believe.

"Quarto! You're back!" squealed a little voice from a platform not too far away.

"Lillo! Yes, I am-dee-wam! But you wouldn't believe where I've been."

"Where?" said the young female elf as she hopped down and ran toward them.

"In Lenora's country, Gepeth-adetha!" Quarto explained.

"No! Fiddlie fee! How did *that* happen?"

"I don't know!"

"That's what we're here to find out," Lenora said.

"Lenora! Coren!"

They looked around to see where the voices were coming from, and there were their old friends Muni and Lero rushing toward them across the square. Hugs were exchanged with the little people, who were delighted to see them again.

"But what are you doing here?" Muni asked.

"I wish I knew," Coren said.

"It was an accident," Lenora added. "We were actually trying to—"

"Another accident!" Lero interrupted. "Isn't it wonderful!"

"I suppose so," Muni said, but she didn't look very convinced.

Accidents? What was Lero talking about?

"And why was Quarto with you?" Lero added. "Was that an accident, too?"

"I suppose it was," Coren said. "You see, somehow he showed up in Lenora's country, Gepeth, out of the blue. And—"

"And let me guess," Muni said, obviously worried, "when he got there, he was a huge giant."

"And caused all sorts of trouble," Lero added.

"How did you know?" Coren asked.

"Because," Muni answered, "it's happening all the time now. The elves are constantly changing size. Why, just yesterday morning one of them got to be so big that she filled the entire square. Caused quite a lot of damage, too."

"And that's not all," Lero said, his face beaming. "All sorts of strange and wonderful things are happening. In fact, they're happening right now. Look—look over there!" He pointed up to the top of one of the high buildings in the square. It had grown a dome, like a cathedral. And now, as the four of them stared up at it, colored light began to pour out of it, like a gigantic rainbow that bent in all directions. One of the beams of light, a blue one, curved down out of the sky and fell onto them, turning them all bright blue.

"That's what it's like here all the time now," said Muni, who looked quite silly trying to be serious with a bright blue face. "And you know, Lenora," she added, "we think it's all your fault."

"My fault? What do you mean?"

"You *are* the one who got rid of Hevak."

"But surely that was a good thing," Lenora objected.

"Don't get me wrong, we'll be grateful to you forever for ridding our land of that monster. But once he was gone, well, we Gragians decided that we'd never let anybody push us around. Ever again. So, we decided on a new rule."

"The new law of Grag, agreed to by everybody," Lero interrupted. "*No* law!"

"No law?" Coren repeated, his face still bright blue even though the colored light had long since disappeared.

"None at all," Lero confirmed. "We have total freedom! And," he added, suddenly turning into six exact duplicates of himself and speaking in unison, "WE LOVE IT!!"

"Some of us love it," Muni interjected. "Some of us, like me, for instance, wonder about it. The minute we agreed to the new law, things started to happen. People began to change.

Everyone not only did whatever they wished, they seemed to *become* whatever they wished. And it's been getting worse. It's almost as if we'd made a hole in the dike, and the water first started to trickle through and then gradually wore the rest of the dike away."

As she spoke, the square beneath their feet filled with water up to their ankles.

"Every single whim or passing fancy somehow becomes real," Muni added. "See?"

She pointed at Lero, who had turned from six people into one and then become a sweet little pink puppy and was jumping at his sister's leg and barking. "I just thought of him as a dog in the back of my mind for a brief instant—and there he is."

"But not for long," trumpeted the elephant the dog had turned into. "Not for long!!!" He reared up on his hind legs and then came down again, splashing them all as his huge feet hit the water.

"So, Lenora," Coren said, finally no longer blue. "Maybe this explains everything. An outbreak of freedom—it all started here in Grag when we got rid of Hevak—and it's been gradually spreading through the rest of the worlds. All the dikes are going down, all the Balances are going away."

"And that's probably why we came here instead of going into the past," Lenora mused. "We wanted to go where we could find an answer to our questions—and so we came here. But this is even worse than we'd imagined, Coren. What can we do? How can we stop it?"

"There's only one way," Coren answered. "We're going to have to get as many powerful minds as we can together in one place—back in Gepeth, perhaps, or maybe even here—and get them all to agree on one way for the world to be. Then, with any luck, if everybody agrees, it'll stay that— Oof!"

He had been beaned on the head by a falling object and knocked to the now dry pavement.

It was King Rayden, falling out of the sky, directly onto Coren. In fact, people were falling out of the sky all over the square. There was Lufa, and with her, a battalion of wise women. And there were ten or fifteen of Rayden's most powerful councillors.

And there was Coren's father, King Arno.

"Coren, my lad," he said. "You here already? Did you fly? And—that dragon, where is it? One minute it's toasting me like a marshmallow with his foul hot breath, and the next—" He gazed around the chaotic scene of the square. "Where are we? What's happening?"

"I, I must have brought you all here with my thought," Coren stuttered.

Suddenly, Rayden, Savet, Lufa, the wise women, and Arno all blinked out of sight. The various Gragians they had knocked over climbed back onto their feet and went on with their bartering and dancing as if nothing had happened.

"Bring them back," Lenora yelled at Coren. "We need them!"

Coren tried, but nothing happened. "I'm sorry," he sighed, "but I can't seem to make it happen again."

"Blast," Lenora said. "But at least the hour will soon be up, and with any luck, they'll bring *us* back to the castle and we can do it there."

"Yes," Coren said, "I guess that's the best we can hope for."

"Too bad, though," Lenora mused. "It would have been fun to go into the past. A lot of fun."

"I suppose so," Coren said. "But if what Muni says is true, then it's clear the cause is right here in Grag—Lenora? Lenora!!"

Lenora could hear Coren's voice as he called her, growing fainter and fainter. She stood alone on a long black road with a yellow line down the middle. There were fields on either side of the road, but no people and no Coren. She was completely alone, again. Where had her mind transported her to now?

25

She willed herself back to Grag and then back home to the castle, but to no avail. She appeared, for the moment, to be stuck here. She stared down the black road and thought about what to do.

In the end, there seemed to be little choice—she had to do something, and the only thing she could do was to walk down the road. Maybe she'd find somebody who could tell her where she was, at least. Anything was better than just standing there.

She didn't know which direction to choose, so she decided to twirl around until she got too dizzy to twirl anymore, then just open her eyes and go in whatever direction she was facing. She twirled and twirled until her head was spinning as fast as her body. Reeling, she fell to the ground, imagining that she was hearing strange voices, confusing noises.

No, she wasn't imagining—she *was* hearing noises. She opened her eyes.

It was the strangest sight she'd ever seen—and she had seen some very strange places.

It was a city, more or less. Or, at least, there were buildings all around her. But they weren't ever the same buildings for more than a moment or two. They kept changing, turning into other buildings, even into other objects. As she watched, a charming cottage, painted pink and with a thatched roof, turned into a gleaming box made of mirrors, and then into a huge tree. So much was happening all around her that she could barely begin to understand it. People were coming and going with frightening speed in front of her, beside her, even over her head. Some seemed to have wings, while others just floated in the air like human-shaped clouds.

As she stared at all of this, Lenora's mind was flooded with images: food, places, smells, emotions. And as she thought of them, she experienced them. One minute she had a turkey sandwich in her hand, the next the sword with which Cori had impaled the giant elf.

Her head hurt. She wished she were somewhere quiet. And she was back on the road again, staring at the green crops.

But only for an instant. No matter how much she wished herself away, she kept finding herself back in the center of the endlessly transforming city.

She was so dazed by it all she barely felt it when a boy tumbled into her. He was wearing clothes that were much too big for him, and he was pushing himself over the smooth black pavement on some kind of board with wheels on it. Apparently, he'd been going too fast to stop.

"Hey," Lenora said as she picked herself up from the hard gray street where she'd fallen. "Why don't you watch where you're going?"

The boy pushed his long hair out of his eyes and gave her a bewildered look.

"Jeez, lady," he said, "are you nuts? This is the twenty-first century, isn't it? Nobody has to watch where they're going."

And then he became a large wheel and rolled off over the hard pavement himself.

The twenty-first century! That was hundreds and hundreds of years ago.

She had done it, then, without even really intending to. She had ended up back in the ancient past.

And there was no question about it, she told herself as a group of people passed by her, all hopping on one leg. She was definitely in a time before the Balance. Hopping like that was the one thing that irked Agneth most of all. He considered it an act of sacrilege against his precious Balance, and he never, ever allowed anyone to do it.

Lenora watched a giant worm ingest a row of houses over to her left and then tried to find something to stand under to avoid the heavy fall of soft red candies that had just begun.

Well, if she was in the past before the Balance, maybe she could discover how they had created the Balance. Then she could return to her own time and they could recreate it again.

But wait, did she really *want* it? Hadn't she always been against the Balance? And now that she knew about the people in the Gepethian countryside—well, maybe she would keep her secret to herself, and recreate it her *own* way.

But first things first. She'd have to see if she could find out what the secret was. And then she'd have to see if she could return home. And then—

She stared at the chaotic scene around her. She really didn't think she'd like to be stuck here. For one thing, it would be impossible to get into trouble or irritate anyone. So far as she could tell, everyone just did as they pleased and no one seemed to care. That was a very disconcerting idea.

Anyway, how could she possibly find out anything from any

of these people—or worms, or trees, or whatever they happened to be? They didn't seem to want to remain one thing long enough for her to ask them a question—let alone have time to give her an answer. And they were giving her a terrible headache. Oh, if only they'd stop shifting around so much.

And they did, right away. Everything suddenly stopped. Even the candies that were still pelting her stopped in midair, hanging suspended as if glued to the sky.

Well, thought Lenora, this is more like it. Maybe now, if I'm not frozen, too, I can get a closer look at things. And since she didn't wish to be frozen, she wasn't. She headed off down the street, carefully investigating everything that she saw, looking for a clue. It was a bit like walking through a very strange painting.

The first thing that caught her eye was a man with a large blue ball instead of a head. No, she could see as she looked more closely, it wasn't a ball. It was a world, a complete miniature world. There were oceans and continents on it, and if she looked closely, she could see mountains and cities beneath the wisps of clouds.

Now there was a man with the world on his shoulders.

Then she noticed two people who were entirely intertwined. They looked sort of like braided rope—you could tell there were two people there, but they were entirely twisted and turned around each other. They must have been in love with each other—either that or someone was torturing them in a very nasty way.

The next person Lenora noticed was a fellow with about a dozen books poised in the air and circled around his head. He had grabbed one of them and was frozen in the act of reading it. Lenora hurried over to take a quick look at the books—she loved to read, and she wondered what kind of books were popular this far back in the past.

It took no effort at all to unfreeze the books, one at a time, take hold of one, and keep everything else frozen.

The first book she skimmed was some kind of fantasy—a boy was traveling to fairy country with the help of a little hat. It looked exciting, but a silly fantasy wasn't going to be much help to someone in *her* situation.

She put that book back over the man's head and glanced at the next one, which was hovering just beside his ear. Another fantasy, about a girl from someplace named Kansas who seemed to have gotten lost. Just like me, Lenora thought—except it's not real.

The book that floated just behind the back of the man's head looked much more promising. The cover said it was a history of the world up until the present. Maybe if she knew about all that she could understand things better. Lenora grabbed the book and began to read.

"Gavortnung," the book said. "Om der fangottelinden, diw bonkateri ist a pombalon."

Drat. It was in a language she didn't understand. Why did it say *History* on the front and then have all this gibberish inside?

But this man could understand it, obviously, or else he wouldn't have it there—she could unfreeze him and ask him to tell her what it said.

She did it. He simply stood there and ignored her as he devoured the words on the page in front of him, while the rest of the books twirled slowly around him.

"Sir," she said, "your book—this history?" She showed him the book she still held in her hand. "Could you tell me what it says?"

He looked up impatiently. "I suppose so," he said. "Or at least, I can tell you what it says when *I* read it." He took the book from her.

"Gavortnung," he began.

"No, no," Lenora interrupted. "I can't understand that language. I was wondering if you could tell me what it means."

He gave her a scornful look. "Now you're just being silly, aren't you? It means whatever you want it to mean, of course."

"What? I don't understand."

"Good heavens, don't you know anything at all? Everyone knows that a book is different every time a different person reads it."

"Oh," Lenora said. "I guess I should have known that. If everyone's allowed to imagine whatever they want, then of course it's only logical. Drat. I did so want to know about history and how things got to be the way they are and all."

"Well, then," the man said impatiently, "why don't you just make it say that? He thrust the open book right in front of her face. "Use your imagination, for goodness' sake."

Lenora had no choice but to look at the page in front of her.

"It's not the same," she said in surprise. "The words are different than they were before!"

"Of course they're different—they're *your* words now, of course—the ones you want to read. Here, take it, if you're too lazy to make up your own." He thrust the book into her hands, and then said, "Honestly, the young people nowadays. Not a jot of gumption. I don't know what the world is coming to!" Then he shook his head and strode off angrily down the street, still reading.

Lenora was too busy reading to even notice. ". . . when everything changed," the book said.

The man was right—it was exactly what she wanted to

know. No question about it, there were certain advantages to being able to make things be what you want them to be. She kept on reading:

> . . . when everything changed. Before then, of course, for centuries, people had been slaves to necessity. Nobody could ever have what they really wanted, for the human race was far too busy gathering food to keep alive and fighting wars to keep its homes safe and protecting itself from the weather.

How awful, Lenora thought. How could people live like that?

> And then, gradually, human ingenuity came to the fore. Products of the human imagination—machines, methods, ideas— made life easier, and made it more possible for people to live as they wanted and do as they wished.
>
> And once the flow started, it swelled and swelled. The inventions continued and grew more sophisticated. By the end of the twentieth century, there were machines that could do anything people did, machines that could read and move of their own volition and even machines that could think. And as those machines grew ever more complex, they gave people increasingly more free- dom—the freedom to be what they wanted, where they wanted. And as the machines

gave human minds increasing freedom,
human minds became increasingly free.
Without the old necessity, all the boring old
restrictions simply disappeared. Free to
think, people thought freely—imagined
whatever they wished and wanted. The
present age of freedom had begun.

So that was what had happened, Lenora thought as she
snapped the book shut. What *is* happening now, in this time.
Nobody has to think about duty or work or putting things off
until a better time—and so their minds are totally free, totally flexible. They are whatever they imagine themselves to be.
They are—all this.

As she looked out over the frantic scene, she let go of her
wish for everything to stop and it all began again. Her eyes
darted this way and that, taking it all in. Now that she under-
stood it better, she could hardly get her fill of it. Total freedom! It was wonderful!

And they gave up all this for the Balance, she thought.
How could they have? She still didn't know that—she might
have to move forward in time until she found out. How could
they possibly have been foolish enough to give up all this?

And yet, as she surveyed the busy scene, she found herself
sensing something disturbing. She watched as a woman changed
the color of her dress about fifteen times in fewer than fifteen seconds, and found herself wondering if people were happier in this
time or in her own. It was a scary thought.

Being able to do whatever you want must get boring after
a while, she thought. Because people here did seem to be
almost—well, almost desperate. There was certainly some-

thing desperate about the way they kept changing all the time. Were they never able to settle down at any one task or keep any one body and just be content?

"Of course not," a voice suddenly spoke inside her head. "I mean, I've tried, sure, I've tried, again and again and again. I imagine myself the most ideal person to be, with every feature I could ever possibly want, and I make myself into it—and then, somehow, I think to myself, Druscindo, this isn't enough, I want to be something different. Because I can still imagine other things, see? Oh, it's very, very frustrating, let me tell you! Actually, I don't like the name Druscindo. Call me Feeflo."

It was obviously one of the people nearby, reading her thoughts and talking to her mentally. But who?

"It's me, over here."

She turned to see a young man—a very plain one, too.

No, a very handsome one. Or rather, he had suddenly become very handsome—dark hair, muscular body, piercing brown eyes. Exactly her idea of a perfectly handsome man. He was even wearing armor.

"There," he said inside her head, "that's better—unless, of course, you've changed your mind?" There was a pause. "No," he said then, clearly surprised, "you haven't changed your mind—you *still* think that this is exactly the way I ought to look. How odd. Because now, myself, I'd much rather look like this. Call me Arminnneoowww."

He changed into a cuddly little white kitten and ran down the street, out of sight.

Poor thing, Lenora thought. Never contented. And she knew, she could tell simply from sensing the atmosphere around her, that all the rest felt exactly the same way.

And so did she—she had totally changed her mind in no time at all. Was it catching? Because she had just been thinking how wonderful this world was, and now she was thinking it was all horrible. She was flowing from one idea to another, one thing to another.

The entire scene shifted, and she found herself floating through a world of water, breathing quite comfortably through the gills in her neck.

26

Lenora heard a loud noise like thunder, and as the water changed back into air, the ever-shifting crowd parted to reveal a group of giant insects hurtling toward her. No, it wasn't insects, it was the nasty men she'd met before, riding on those metal machines that looked like dragonflies. Now there were four of them, though. The one in front was a stranger to Lenora, much shorter than the rest but dressed as they were in a black shiny jacket. Lenora couldn't see the leader's face because of a shiny mushroom-shaped mask that covered his entire head.

"Okay," the leader shouted in a surprisingly high-pitched voice as the thunderous noise suddenly switched off. "Here she is, finally. You fellows sit there and keep your mouths shut until I tell you otherwise."

"Yes, boss."

"Whatever you say, Sayley."

Sayley? As Lenora looked at the short rider more closely, he removed the mushroom from his head. No, *she* removed it—it *was* Sayley, all right. What was she doing here?

"Leteshia!" Sayley said, "I've been looking for you everywhere!"

"How on earth did you get here?" Lenora asked.

"I don't know," Sayley answered. "I missed you in the castle. I mean, they were nice to me, of course, but they were all so busy that no one really paid any attention to me, and I started wishing I was where you were and suddenly I was here—but not with you, with them." And she pointed to the three men in their leather jackets.

Lenora glared at Sayley's traveling companions. "They didn't try to hurt you or anything, did they? If these bullies tried to hurt you—"

Sayley laughed. "I don't think so," she said, a bit of a nasty gleam in her eye. "You wouldn't hurt me, boys, would you?"

The three practically groveled.

"No, never, Sayley, never!"

"Or my friend Leteshia?"

"Never, never."

Lenora couldn't even begin to imagine what Sayley had done to make them so obedient. She suspected it was better not to know.

"But, Sayley," Lenora said, "you must realize by now that I'm the Princess Lenora. Why do you keep on calling me Leteshia?"

"I don't know," Sayley answered. "That's the way I've always thought of you, I guess. May I please keep calling you that?"

Lenora sighed. "I suppose," she said. Although, she thought, it's obvious the child is quite capable of doing whatever she wants, including calling me by my correct name. She's just so stubborn!

And then Lenora realized that she was feeling about Sayley the way people must feel about her. That softened her, and she smiled at Sayley, who took it as a yes and continued talking.

"Oh, Leteshia, we've been having so much fun! These

motorcycle things are such a blast! That's what they're called, motorcycles! You can go real fast on them! And everyone runs to get out of your way! And you know what else, Leteshia? I've got one of these fantastic shooters, all for myself! See?" She reached into her shiny jacket and pulled out one of the weapons that had so frightened Lenora earlier. "Look!"

She pointed the weapon at a large balloon that was passing overhead, tied to a basket with a group of children in it. BAM! There was a tremendously loud noise, and as Lenora watched, the balloon deflated, air hissing out of a large tear in its side.

"Blast," one of the children in the basket said, and then he and the others turned into geese and flew off in a flock. The empty basket sunk to the ground, just missing Lenora's head.

"Isn't it wonderful?" Sayley said, again turning to Lenora.

"It *is* dangerous," Lenora objected.

"Oh, Leteshia, don't be silly! I never shoot it at people—not on purpose anyway. Do I?" Again she turned to her group.

"No, Sayley."

"Of course not, Sayley."

"And I don't let *them* shoot it at people, either. And even if I do accidentally make a hole in somebody, I can just imagine it isn't there, and it isn't!" She paused, and her face grew serious. "It's a good thing, too, because I don't like the blood, really. And neither do my gang."

"That's right, Sayley."

"Blood is bad, Sayley."

Just then, the sky darkened. It wasn't a cloud, though. It was Quarto, the elf, even bigger than before, hurtling toward them, about to crush them all.

"Don't worry, my people," a strong male voice called from a platform down the street. Why, it looked like Hevak, the

Gragian leader. But it couldn't be, he was dead.

But now they were standing in a square that looked like the old Grag, before it changed.

"I will call out the platoons!" Hevak called. And even as he spoke, a group of flying machines appeared over the buildings and buzzed toward Quarto, loud bangs filling the air.

Luckily for Quarto, he had begun to shrink, and he was soon small enough to drop through the projectiles unscathed.

As he landed on the ground, the square shifted again. Now there was a river flowing by and a domed cathedral on an island in it. Near it, a tall, towerlike structure of webbed steel thrust into the sky—and then, as Lenora watched, it grew into a huge mountain.

"Watch out," her father's voice said, and he pushed her aside, just in time to avoid being crushed by a huge rolling stone. It was coming from the mountain that now occupied the site of the steel tower. It was a volcano erupting!

"What are *you* doing here, Father?" Lenora said, as she stood plastered against a building and watched huge rocks roll by on what looked like a stream of hot lava.

"I don't know, dear," Rayden said, shaking his head. "It seems that things are getting even more disrupted all the time. Times and places are all getting mixed up together now. Why, before I came here, I was in a strange, round wooden building, with hundreds of people staring at me, and I was dressed in a black garment that showed off my legs and holding a human skull and shouting at all the people about how I knew the person once before he died, in some place called York. Isn't that strange?"

"Very strange, indeed, Rayden," Queen Savet said. "I hope you washed your hands after." As she spoke, hundreds of towels descended from overhead, all singing together.

"♪ Wash your hands, ♪ wash your hands, ♪ wash your haaaaanndssss," the towels sang.

One fell on the man with the books rotating around his head, who was now strolling across the square again, still reading. The towel covered both his head and the book in front of it.

"Hmph," he said coolly, as he removed it, looking over at Lenora. "The weather is particularly unsettled today, isn't it?"

"I don't *want* those towels here," Sayley wailed from behind Lenora. "Go away, go away, go away!" Her voice sounded strangely wooden. Lenora turned to see that Sayley was now a tree—the voice was coming from a hole in her trunk.

And it had no effect on the towels, which just kept right on descending, filling up the surface of the street. As one of the towels fell over Lenora's head, it shifted, and now her head was draped with a gooey cake covered in whipped cream.

"Mmm," a voice said. "Much better than towels. Hi, Lenora."

Yes, now Lero was there, too, and Muni, and a number of Gepethian trolls and elves.

"Her name is Leteshia!" the tree howled loudly, "LETESHIA!!!"

The buildings suddenly turned to clear glass, and through them, on the next street, Lenora was almost sure that she could see a large green dragon, breathing fire. Standing under its flames, holding a sword, and looking very fierce, was Coren. Or maybe it was Cori—he had on a suit of armor. It was hard to tell, because the street was so full of people and creatures of all shapes and sizes that she couldn't even see the glass buildings anymore.

Was everybody in the entire universe going to suddenly

show up here in this street? Or riverbank, or whatever it was? And then blink out again, the way her father and mother had? And where were Lero and Muni? Was that them over there— that pair of tall blue vases on top of which Quarto was perched?

And now, her thoughts were feeling so scattered—she couldn't seem to keep them together. It felt as if her head was exploding, as if little bits of it were flying off into the void. She raised her hands to her forehead and ran them through her long blonde hair in desperation.

And now, her thoughts were feeling so scattered—she couldn't seem to keep them together. It felt as if her head was exploding, as if little bits of it were flying off into the void. She raised her hands to her forehead and ran them through her long blonde hair in desperation.

I must be going mad, she thought, it's unbearable, completely unbearable.

My hair is feeling kind of grimy, she thought. Time for a shampoo—and a good bath.

This is actually kind of fun, she thought, I feel so free, so creative, so full of different ideas!

Oh, thought Lenora, this is too much. It's just all too confusing, I can hardly think.

Oh, thought Lenora, this is too much. It's just all too confusing, I can hardly think.

Oh, thought Lenora, this is too much. It's just all too confusing, I can hardly think.

Oh, thought Lenora, this is too much. It's just all too confusing, I can hardly think.

Oh, thought Lenora, this is too much. It's just all too confusing, I can hardly think.

Oh, thought Lenora, this is too much. It's just all too confusing, I can hardly think.

"STOP IT!"

She had screeched before she even realized she was doing it, so loud that it had actually been heard by everybody through all of their different imaginings and wishes. They all stood, stopped in midgesture, staring at her.

"What's wrong, Leteshia?" the tree said into the silence.

"I'm sorry, Sayley," Lenora said, "but I can't take it anymore. Why can't everybody agree on *one* reality for a change?"

"Agree?" the crowd murmured.

"One reality?"

They stood in silence, clearly astonished by the idea.

Finally, the man with the book in front of his face spoke. "Agreement—how innovative! How refreshing! An excellent idea!"

"Excellent, excellent," the crowd murmured.

"And," the man with the books continued, "I know exactly what we should agree on. Silence at all hours, and compulsory literacy!"

"Nonsense," a man with three mouths said, "I hate reading. I like eating. We'll make everybody and everything edible."

"No, we'll all live underwater," someone else shouted.

"I want everything green," another voice added.

"I want to be in charge of everything," Sayley demanded.

Then they all started shouting at one another. Lenora couldn't stand it. She felt like her head was going to *burst*. Suddenly, Gepeth seemed so quiet, so peaceful, so wonderful. A picture of it formed in her mind, everyone with their job to do, the order, the blue skies, the happy singing, the serenity . . .

It had become strangely quiet. Everyone was staring at her. And since she could read their minds, she realized that somehow they had all been reading *her* mind. The image of Gepeth she'd been seeing was bouncing back at her from every direction. It must have been so strong that she'd sent it out, or pulled everyone in . . .

"I like it!" said the bookworm. "I could read peacefully all day!"

"I like it, too," nodded another.

"Me, too!"

Lenora shook her head. "No, wait," she said, "you don't understand. It's not perfect there. Lots of people—"

But she was cut off. And Coren filled her mind. "Lenora," he called, "Lenora, come back."

He was pulling her somehow, pulling her toward him. She felt herself moving.

"Wait!" she cried. "Not yet. I have to warn them about—"

But it was too late. She was already back.

She was in Gepeth, in the castle, staring into Coren's deep blue eyes. He put his hand to her cheek and smiled.

"I pulled you back, Lenora," said a voice behind her—her father's voice. "Just as I said I would. After Coren found you, of course. He seems to be connected to you in a very strong way—if he weren't you'd have been lost forever in that crazy place we all just tumbled into and out of a while back. Well, thank goodness, I say—and we'd better get this wedding ceremony moving along."

Lenora, still dazed, looked around her. Yes, she was in the conference room in Gepeth. Her mother was there, too, along with Coren and her father, as were Lufa and Agneth. No volcanoes. No giants or elves. No wise women. No chickens. No towels.

She was indeed home—and things seemed to be back to normal.

27

"What's happened?" Lenora said, bewildered.

"Somehow," Lufa said, "the Balance has been restored."

"Yes," Rayden nodded, "it's true. I can feel it. The Balance is back. I must go see about that giant—let's hope he's gone." And he bustled over to the window.

Lenora sensed immediately that her father was right. She had her powers—she could feel them humming away inside her. But she also felt totally in control of them.

"Are you all right, Lenora?" It was Coren. He was looking at her anxiously.

"Yes, I am. But you know, I'm a little worried. Father pulled me out just when—"

"The giant *is* gone!" King Rayden announced.

"Actually," said Coren, "he's been gone for quite a while." And he smiled at Lenora.

"How did you get back here?" Lenora asked Coren, as she remembered that the last time she'd seen him had been in Grag.

"Your father brought me back," Coren replied. "Right

on schedule. But then we couldn't find you. Where *were* you? What *was* that place?"

Just then the door opened, and Agneth burst in, carrying a huge, dusty old book.

"I have performed the Rituals," he announced. "I am cleansed. The Recordings are here, and I may read them to you. Our solution is at hand!"

"Well, actually, Agneth," Rayden said after an embarrassing silence, "I believe we've had our solution already. Hadn't you noticed?"

Agneth looked around the room, surprised. "My goodness," he finally said, "I—I do believe you're right. How strange. How wonderful."

"So you might as well just put that dusty old book away, and let's have a party to celebrate!"

"Oh, no, your majesty," Agneth said, "I could not do that. No. The Balance wouldn't allow it. Why, who knows what might happen—the same confusion all over again, perhaps. No, once the cleansing has occurred, the book must be read."

Rayden sighed.

"Well, if it must be done, it must—proceed."

Agneth brought the book over to the table and reverently laid it down, opened it, and cleared his throat.

"I shall now read from the Precious Recordings," he said. "Praise the Balance!"

"Praise the Balance," everyone else mumbled.

Agneth once more cleared his throat, and then read in a loud clear voice:

And it came to pass that freedom descended

upon the land, and all places were as one place, and all times were as one time, and the people did dwell in chaos.

"And, oh!" the voice of the people called, "oh, for an end to chaos! Oh, for a world of order! Let us agree!"

And then were their prayers answered. The divine Leteshia did appear before her people, all in shining light, a rock in the midst of the shift-ings. And then she did imagine for them a per-fect world. And they found it to be perfect.

And peace and order ruled in the land.

Lenora stared at Agneth. For a moment, she couldn't catch her breath. Leteshia. The perfect world. Her knees buckled and she sank down into a chair.

Coren was at her side instantly. "Lenora, Lenora, what is it?"

"It was me, Coren," she whispered in an agonized voice. "It was me. I imagined being back here in Gepeth, the palace, the quiet, and they all liked the idea so much, and Father pulled me away before I could tell them all the problems, show them that not everyone *is* happy, how mad it all makes me . . ."

Coren's jaw dropped. The room was so silent you could hear only Lenora's ragged gasps for air.

"Are you telling me," Coren said, "that it was *you—you* cre-ated the Balance?"

"Yes," said Lenora, "it was me."

EPILOGUE

Lenora and Coren sat with Fullbright looking at arrangements of flowers for corsages. It was as if nothing had happened—and yet it was really only hours since everything had returned to normal. Why, the messenger Lenora had sent off to find out if Sayley had come back safely had just returned with the good news that the little girl was home, indeed—that she'd suddenly appeared right in the middle of the bread dough her mother was rolling out, and that she had been sent to bed without her supper. Lenora wondered what goodies Sayley was thinking up in the darkness of her bedroom at this very moment.

Well, whatever it was, it hadn't disturbed the Balance here in the castle—not yet, at least.

"Now," Fullbright chattered, "these yellow ones would be simply perfect for the female guests, Princess, don't you think? Princess?"

"Whatever," Lenora said, waving her hand. She turned to Coren. "It's not fair," she exclaimed. "It's not fair! How am I ever going to be able to complain again, now that everyone knows it was me!"

Lenora stared at Coren, waiting for an answer, but he seemed to be hiding his face behind his hand.

"Coren! Coren!" She tugged his hand free.

He was laughing. He was turning red, he was laughing so hard! "Stop that! It isn't funny!"

"Uh, Princess, about the choreography?" Fullbright was desperately trying to get her attention. The wedding was fast approaching, and all the decisions he'd made so carefully with Leni now had to be remade all over again.

"Choreography?" Lenora snapped. "Oh, everyone can dance a jig down the aisle, as far as I'm concerned." She glared at Coren. "*What* is so funny?"

Coren doubled over. "I can't help it," he gasped between shouts of laughter. "It's too funny. *You've* created the entire universe, practically. And you hate it!"

"But it was an accident! I didn't really want things that way. Well, maybe I did, for a moment, but—oh, nothing ever works out the way you expect."

Coren continued to laugh.

Lenora felt herself smile, just a little. After all, it really was too silly, wasn't it? All these years, railing against the Balance, and whose fault had the whole thing been?

And the silliest thing was, it wasn't really an accident. For all her complaining, she did love her home, despite all its annoying faults. For a moment there, she'd *wanted* it, so much that nothing else mattered. And she certainly liked it better than that crazy world of the past, where there was so much freedom you could hardly even think straight.

And where your thoughts became real instantly. Even disastrous thoughts like *that* one.

She began to laugh, too. She and Coren were soon guffawing uproariously and rolling around on Fullbright's carpet.

Fullbright threw up his hands in disgust. "You know," he said, "some of us take our work seriously!"

That brought Lenora up short. And her seriousness immediately got Coren's attention.

"Just because I created it," Lenora said, panting, "doesn't mean I have to like it. Yes, sure, it's better than that awful chaos back then, but it certainly isn't perfect. What about all the people who are unhappy, the ones who have the Balance forced on them against their will? If it's all my fault, then I have an even greater responsibility. It's up to me to try to make things right! As soon as possible!" She began to rise to her feet.

"Now, Lenora," Coren warned, grabbing her hand and pulling her back onto the carpet. "Everything is back to normal, finally. Let's not mess with it, please."

"But, Coren—"

"Please." He held firmly onto her hand. "Oh, and speaking of normal, I forgot to tell you. I spoke to my father an hour or so ago, and it seems that the Balance returned in Andilla at exactly the same time it did here. All is as it was there—except for the addition of two people. Cori and Leni."

Lenora stopped trying to tug her hand away and turned to him. "Cori and Leni are still in Andilla?"

Coren nodded. "And apparently loving it. Leni spends all her time imagining dresses and hairdos without having to worry about disrupting the Balance or doing anything to annoy anybody, and Cori gets to slay dragons at will just by thinking them up inside his head. According to my mother, he imagines some pretty impressive dragons—she loves to watch, my father says. Yes, my parents love them both." He grinned. "I think they like *him* more than *me*."

"Nonsense," Lenora said. "Of course they don't. But I suppose it's harmless to leave them there—for the moment. And I couldn't think them away again, could I? It'd be like that dead horse of Sayley's. I guess your folks are stuck with them for a while." Her face changed. "But tell me, Coren, what did you mean when you said the Balance came back to Andilla? I didn't know you had the Balance there, too."

"I didn't know it either, before. I didn't realize that's what it was, because in Andilla we don't call it the Balance. But we have it anyway. Everybody has it. Every country has its own way of making sure things stay the way they are. That's what I meant when I said you practically created the entire universe."

"But—"

"I asked Agneth about it. It seems that, back in the past, after the divine Leteshia made her famous appearance, some people wanted to keep some of their imaginings—the things they especially liked to do. Some of them wanted to keep on reading thoughts, some wanted to say everything in poetry, some wanted to be fish living under the sea. The Kitznoldians couldn't give up their green thumbs and their magical ways with crops of all sorts. So everyone finally agreed that they'd create special places, different countries where people who wanted to do different things could just go ahead and do them. That's why each country now has its own special talent—and its own special rules about what you can or can't do to keep the Balance, or the Equilibrium, or whatever they happen to call it. That's why I wanted to leave Andilla in the first place—there, the law makes everybody read thoughts, just as Agneth here stops people from doing it—and back home, making what you think real is *against* the law. You actually didn't know that?"

"I've never been all that interested in reality," Lenora said in a small voice. Then, for a moment, she sat on the carpet in thoughtful silence.

"It's worse than I thought," she said finally. "Much worse. I have to get busy! There's so much to tackle. There's still that mess going on in Grag."

"So far as we know," said Coren. He paused. "I wonder why everything *has* returned to normal, just because of something you did hundreds of years in the past."

"Well, to me is was only hours ago," Lenora said. "So it wasn't the past, it was the present."

Coren stared at her. "That makes my head hurt," he sighed.

"We don't have time to worry about things like that," Lenora said, rising to her feet. "After all, the Balance is still too strict here. And *I* have to fix it!"

"But Lenora," Coren warned her, also getting on his feet, "they loosened the Balance in Grag, remember? And that's what led to all this mess. In fact, if things are still the same in Grag, couldn't this mess start all over again?"

"Exactly!" Lenora agreed. "But there's got to be a way. There's got to be some way in between, a way that isn't as totally controlled as your country or mine, *or* as totally free as Grag. Some—"

Coren completed the sentence for her. "Some Balance?" he said.

The two of them looked at each other and started to laugh again.

"Princess," Fullbright said. "The centerpieces?"

Lenora drew herself up to full height. "Master Fullbright," she said, "if you imagine that I am going to sit here and worry about corsages and centerpieces when I have an entire world to set straight, then you had better reconsider."

"Lenora, please, please, just leave everything," Coren urged. "People will work things out for themselves."

"Don't be silly, Coren," she said. "I made it. I can fix it." And she stomped purposefully out of the room, muttering something about using all the power she could get and maybe asking Sayley if she'd like to join her in a little adventure.

Coren stared after her. Well, that was life with Lenora. Never dull.

He shrugged an apology to Fullbright and hurried off to help Lenora save the world.

ABOUT THESE POINT FANTASY AUTHORS

CAROL MATAS and PERRY NODELMAN are the co–authors of *More Minds* and its predecessor *Of Two Minds*, also published by Point Fantasy.

CAROL MATAS has written numerous books for children and young adults, including *After the War*, *Lisa's War*, *Daniel's Story*, and *Sworn Enemies*. *Lisa's War* was listed as a Notable Book of the Year in the *New York Times Book Review* and as a Young Adults' Choice by the International Reading Association. Matas lives in Winnipeg, Canada, with her husband and two children.

PERRY NODELMAN is the author of *The Same Place But Different*. Nodelman lives in Winnipeg, Canada, with his wife and three children. He teaches English at the University of Winnipeg.

Fantastic Journeys to Other Worlds...

POINT FANTASY

☐ BCP45759-4	**Princess Nevermore** *Dian Curtis Regan*	$4.50
☐ BCP45896-5	**Shadow of the Red Moon** *Walter Dean Myers*	$4.50
☐ BCP97218-9	**Book of Enchantments** *Patricia C. Wrede*	$4.50
☐ BCP45722-5	**Enchanted Forest Chronicles, Book One:** **Dealing with Dragons** *Patricia C. Wrede*	$4.50
☐ BCP45721-7	**Enchanted Forest Chronicles, Book Two:** **Searching for Dragons** *Patricia C. Wrede*	$4.50
☐ BCP48467-2	**Enchanted Forest Chronicles, Book Three:** **Calling on Dragons** *Patricia C. Wrede*	$4.50
☐ BCP48475-3	**Enchanted Forest Chronicles, Book Four:** **Talking to Dragons** *Patricia C. Wrede*	$4.50

Send orders to Scholastic Inc., P.O. Box 7500, Jefferson City, MO 65102

Please send me the books I have checked above. I am enclosing $_____ (please add $2.00 to cover shipping and handling). Send check or money order — no cash or C.O.D.s please.

Please allow four to six weeks for delivery. Offer good in the U.S.A. only. Sorry, mail orders are not available to residents in Canada. Prices subject to change.

Name_____ Birthdate ___/___/___
   First   Last   M   D   Y

Address_____

City_____ State_____ Zip_____

Telephone (   ) _____ ☐ Boy ☐ Girl

Where did you buy this book? ☐ Bookstore ☐ Book Fair ☐ Book Club ☐ Other

FAN697

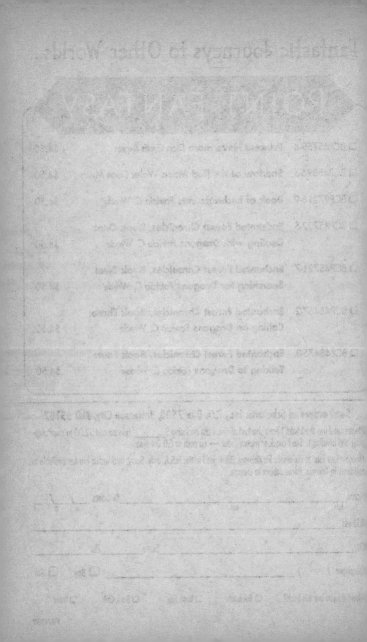